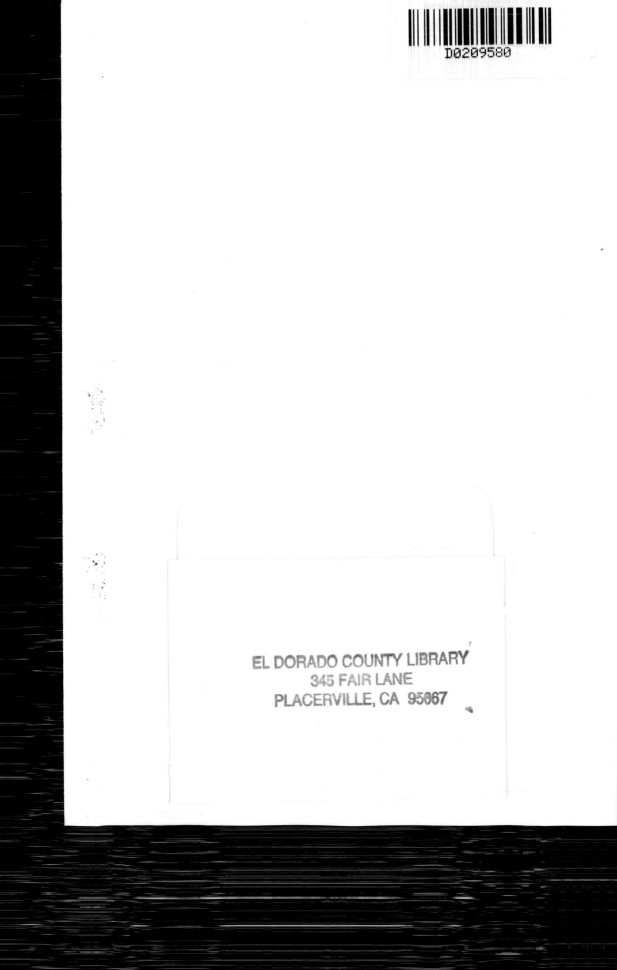

Anne McCaffrey

The People to Know Series

Madeleine Albright
0-7660-1143-7

Neil Armstrong
0-89490-828-6

Isaac Asimov
0-7660-1031-7

Robert Ballard
0-7660-1147-X

Barbara Bush
0-89490-350-0

Willa Cather
0-89490-980-0

Bill Clinton
0-89490-437-X

Hillary Rodham Clinton
0-89490-583-X

Bill Cosby
0-89490-548-1

Walt Disney
0-89490-694-1

Bob Dole
0-89490-825-1

Marian Wright Edelman
0-89490-623-2

Bill Gates
0-89490-824-3

Ruth Bader Ginsberg
0-89490-621-6

John Glenn
0-7660-1532-7

Jane Goodall
0-89490-827-8

Al Gore
0-7660-1232-8

Tipper Gore
0-7660-1142-9

Billy Graham
0-7660-1533-5

Alex Haley
0-89490-573-2

Tom Hanks
0-7660-1436-3

Ernest Hemingway
0-89490-979-7

Ron Howard
0-89490-981-9

Steve Jobs
0-7660-1536-X

Helen Keller
0-7660-1530-0

John F. Kennedy
0-89490-693-3

Stephen King
0-7660-1233-6

John Lennon
0-89490-702-6

Maya Lin
0-89490-499-X

Jack London
0-7660-1144-5

Malcolm X
0-89490-435-3

Wilma Mankiller
0-89490-498-1

Branford Marsalis
0-89490-495-7

Anne McCaffrey
0-7660-1151-8

Barbara McClintock
0-89490-983-5

Rosie O'Donnell
0-7660-1148-8

Gary Paulsen
0-7660-1146-1

Christopher Reeve
0-7660-1149-6

Ann Richards
0-89490-497-3

Sally Ride
0-89490-829-4

Will Rogers
0-89490-695-X

Franklin D. Roosevelt
0-89490-696-8

Steven Spielberg
0-89490-697-6

John Steinbeck
0-7660-1150-X

Martha Stewart
0-89490-984-3

Amy Tan
0-89490-699-2

Alice Walker
0-89490-620-8

Andy Warhol
0-7660-1531-9

Simon Wiesenthal
0-89490-830-8

Elie Wiesel
0-89490-428-0

Frank Lloyd Wright
0-7660-1032-5

People to Know

Anne McCaffrey
Science Fiction Storyteller

Martha P. Trachtenberg

Enslow Publishers, Inc.

40 Industrial Road	PO Box 38
Box 398	Aldershot
Berkeley Heights, NJ 07922	Hants GU12 6BP
USA	UK

http://www.enslow.com

For Thomas Gagnier Griffith,
whose love and support made
this dream—and others—come true.

Library of Congress Cataloging-in-Publication Data

Trachtenberg, Martha P.
    Anne McCaffrey : science fiction storyteller / Martha P. Trachtenberg.
        p. cm. — (People to know)
    Includes bibliographical references and index.
    ISBN 0-7660-1151-8
    1. McCaffrey, Anne—Juvenile literature. 2. Novelists, American—20th century—
Biography—Juvenile literature. 3. Science fiction—Authorship—Juvenile
literature. [1. McCaffrey, Anne—Juvenile literature. 2. Authors, American.
3. Women—Biography.] I. Title. II. Series.
PS3563.A255 Z89   2001
813'.54—dc21
                                                    00-010952

Printed in the United States of America

10 9 8 7 6 5 4 3 2 1

To Our Readers:
All Internet Addresses in this book were active and appropriate when we went to press.
Any comments or suggestions can be sent by e-mail to Comments@enslow.com or to
the address on the back cover.

Illustration Credits: © Corel Corporation, p. 33; © Orla Callaghan,
Wicklow, Ireland, p. 94; Courtesy of Anne McCaffrey, pp. 16, 21, 23, 39, 41,
44, 47, 53, 60, 63, 69, 73, 77, 79, 81, 84; Enslow Publishers, Inc., p. 90;
Jay A. Klein photo courtesy of Anne McCaffrey, p. 11; Photo © Irene Graham
2000, courtesy of Alec Johnson, p. 87; Photo by Chris Hawley, courtesy of
Anne McCaffrey, p. 8.

Cover Illustration: Edmund Ross, Dublin, Ireland

Contents

Acknowledgments

I've been reading Anne McCaffrey's books since her son, Alec, sold me *Dragonflight* and *Dragonquest*. I had wandered into the bookstore he managed in Cambridge, Massachusetts, and asked him to recommend something from the science fiction section.

Twenty-five years later, here is *Anne McCaffrey: Science Fiction Storyteller*. I cannot thank Anne enough; without her help, this book would be a good, *short* essay. I started out admiring her writing; now I admire *her*. And even though I have read them all repeatedly, her books still have the power to keep me up reading when I should be asleep. I call it being McCaffreyed.

All three of her children were equally generous with their time and assistance. My deep gratitude goes to Alec Johnson, Todd J. McCaffrey, and Gigi Kennedy.

Marilyn Alm and her fellow WizOps at CompuServe's online Pern forum tracked down random bits of information. Alm and Lefford Lowden read my manuscript and saved me from a number of what would have been embarrassing errors.

Jody Lynn Nye somehow found time to answer my questions about her collaborations with Anne, and her story of their first meeting is one of my favorites in the entire book.

Harlan Ellison and Robert Silverberg set the scene for Anne's first Hugo Award. Ellison called twice to talk about McCaffrey, and as a longtime Ellison fan I found it stunning to be talking to him. Well, listening, mostly.

My thanks also go to Rachel Brûlé, my honorary niece and early researcher; Jane Knowles, the archivist at Radcliffe College; Laura Mann and Curt Phillips, who helped with online research; Melissa Ann Singer and Ginger Clark at Tor Books; Shelly Shapiro, Anne's editor at Del Rey/Ballantine Books; and writer Ted White. The reference librarians at the Northport and East Northport, New York, libraries always rose with grace and great skill to whatever challenges I presented.

Edmund Ross has my gratitude for permission to use his wonderful photograph of Anne on the cover.

I am very grateful to—and for—my family. My parents, Frances and Morton Trachtenberg, provided love, baby-sitting, catering, and support. My brother, author Jeffrey Trachtenberg, has always encouraged me to write and assured me I could handle an entire book.

Tom Griffith, my husband, and Michael Griffith, my son, deserve more thanks than will fit here.

Last but not least, I thank you, the reader. I hope this book will make you want to read Anne's work, and I do believe you will enjoy it every bit as much as I do.

"My life has NOT been boring."

–Anne McCaffrey

And the Winner Is . . .

It was Sunday night, September 1, 1968. Science fiction writers from around the country had gathered at the Claremont Hotel in Oakland, California. They were hoping to receive a Hugo, an award given by the World Science Fiction Society.

Among them was Anne McCaffrey. Her book *Weyr Search* was up for Best Novella—short novel—and she was having a fine time. Many of her peers, however, were not.

The hotel was a huge Victorian building. Some of the visitors called it the Transylvania Hilton. The awards were given in the banquet hall, which the evening's master of ceremonies, writer Robert Silverberg, later described as a "giant room, pillars everywhere . . . impossible to see much from the audience and (because of poor ventilation) pretty hard to breathe, too." To make matters worse, the sound system failed, and the awards could not be presented until it was fixed. "We were all badly frayed by the time it was under way," Silverberg said.[1]

The attendees had been served a full dinner and listened to a long speech by guest of honor Philip José Farmer. They had waited through what felt like an endless procession of awards—Best Fan Artist, Best Fanzine, Best Fan Writer, Best Dramatic Presentation, Best Professional Magazine, Best Short Story, and Best Novelette—along with all the winners' acceptance speeches. Toes were tapping all over the room, but not Anne McCaffrey's. "I entertained no idea at all that *Weyr Search* would win," she said later. "Actually, folks had been hinting but . . . I simply didn't consider that winning was a possibility."[2]

At last they reached the Best Novella category. McCaffrey was sitting near fellow nominee David Gerrold. He was enjoying the recent success of a *Star Trek* episode he had written, "The Trouble with Tribbles." In later years it proved to be one of *Star Trek*'s most popular shows. As the list of nominees was read, they held hands and listened intently.[3] The competition included some top names in science fiction: Philip José Farmer, Keith Laumer, Roger Zelazny, Samuel R. Delany, and Robert Silverberg.

Silverberg announced a tie for Best Novella. The winners were Philip José Farmer for *Riders of the Purple Wage* and Anne McCaffrey for *Weyr Search*. The audience began to applaud, and McCaffrey made her way to the podium. As writer Harlan Ellison—who

Anne McCaffrey in the mid-1960s.

had three Hugos of his own—handed the Hugo to McCaffrey, she awarded him a big hug and kiss.[4]

Silverberg later remarked, "Annie was enormously excited when she came up, flushed and breathing hard. . . . and after the usual thanks she pointed out something that none of us had realized—that this was the first time a woman had won a Hugo. In those prefeminist days nobody even stopped to consider such statistics; but Annie had."[5]

McCaffrey was elated, and when her friends Betty and Ian Ballantine, the founders of Ballantine Books, later insisted that she fly home first-class with them, she questioned whether she would really need a plane to fly.[6]

What she could not know then was that her

award-winning story would turn into a series of best-sellers. They would be translated into more than twenty languages—including Dutch, French, German, Italian, Japanese, Polish, Portuguese, Spanish, and Swedish—and would be sold around the world. The song lyrics she had written as part of the stories would be set to music and recorded by a pair of young musicians, Tania Opland and Mike Freeman, in Washington State. And she never could have predicted that the next millennium would see the production of a television series, *Dragonriders of Pern*®, based on a short novel rapped out on an old typewriter one spring afternoon.

*   *   *   *   *   *   *   *

It was hardly an overnight success. McCaffrey had been writing and sending out stories since the early 1950s. "I had rejection slip after rejection slip. I could have papered a wall with them! It was a little discouraging."[7] In 1953, McCaffrey finally made her first sale, a short story called "Freedom of the Race," to *Science Fiction Plus*. "That was my first published story. What a thrill it was. I had a young baby at home, but this production was almost more important."[8]

In 1968, there were very few women writing science fiction—at least, not many writing under their own names. Some used men's names, others used only their initials to mask their female identities. Science fiction still tended to lean heavily on its science content, as it had since the genre began in the 1800s. As McCaffrey explained in an essay in 1974, "In the beginning, and start with the classics of Jules Verne and H. G. Wells, s-f stories were written for a predominantly male audience; the premise being that the female mind was unequipped to cope with science."[9] Far more was written about spaceships and their hardware than about the people—almost always men—inside them. The women who did appear tended to be helpless and usually needed to be rescued from bug-eyed aliens.

McCaffrey, however, had no intention of disguising her identity. "If they weren't going to buy the story under the name of Anne McCaffrey, I wouldn't have let them print it."[10] And McCaffrey was well equipped to cope with science. She took courses in physics and consulted with specialists to make sure her science fiction was based on science facts.[11]

More than that, though, she said, "I was lucky. No one ever mentioned to me that science fiction had a predominantly male readership. No one told me women weren't supposed to write science fiction. I entered the field in the mid-sixties when readers started looking for more viable plots and better characterization, when *Star Trek* had broadened the readership base."[12]

Readers familiar with McCaffrey's work know that personal relationships are almost always at the heart of her tales, but she said that "prior to the sixties, stories with any sort of a love interest were very rare."[13] Anne McCaffrey was one of the writers whose work changed the definition, the boundaries, of science fiction.

But in 1968, that was all yet to come.

In the Beginning

Anne Inez McCaffrey was born on April 1, 1926, in Cambridge, Massachusetts. Her parents, George Herbert McCaffrey and Anne Dorothy McElroy McCaffrey, already had one child, Hugh. When Anne was three months old, her father got a job as chief researcher for the New York City Commerce and Industry Association, and the family moved to Montclair, New Jersey. Her younger brother, Kevin, was born a year later.

George McCaffrey, the son of an Irish policeman from Boston, Massachusetts, had received his college degree *magna cum laude* (with great honors) and earned a master's degree and Ph.D. in government from Harvard University. Anne's mother had worked as an advertising copywriter in Boston before her marriage. She could not afford to attend college full-time, but she took courses whenever she could. Over her years of study, she learned to speak French, Russian, Japanese, and Thai.

Anne's maternal grandmother lived with the McCaffreys until her death in 1939. She had been a schoolteacher, and her husband had worked as a printer-engraver. Anne McCaffrey later described her grandmother as a "rather petty tyrant . . . certain that her daughter had married beneath her, and never failing to make my father aware of this opinion."[1]

Anne's parents were not typical of their generation. Men generally supported—and ran—their families. The women stayed home, kept house, raised the children, and went along with their husbands' wishes. George McCaffrey was not the standard husband, though. After he fought in World War I, which ended in 1918, he remained overseas to serve as a military-government officer in Poland. When he came back to the United States, he stayed active in the Army Reserves. This meant that he was away from home for part of every summer for military service. He did not fit the mold of many other husbands in suburban New Jersey.

George McCaffrey was very much a soldier, and his friends and family referred to him as "the Colonel." His children were used to a military touch when they spent time with him. He did not play tag with them in the backyard. Instead, he taught all his children to perform close-order drills—marching in formation—and made sure they all knew how to *run*. The neighborhood kids sometimes teased the McCaffrey children about their father's "parade-ground" voice. He could be heard three blocks away when he called them home. Anne McCaffrey later said that it set them apart from the other kids, and they took pride in being different. Still, it was not easy being the Colonel's child. He was a perfectionist in all aspects of their lives. Anne and her brothers sometimes grumbled about "manicuring the ants' toenails" while they worked in the garden under his close supervision. There was always something else to tidy up, to trim, to make right.[2]

Anne and her younger brother, Kevin, play with their mother in the backyard of their home in Montclair, New Jersey.

Anne's mother, too, was not a traditional stay-at-home wife and mother. She had a lifelong passion for travel, and when Anne was in early elementary school her mother took some trips without the rest of the family. The children were cared for by their grandmother and a series of live-in housekeepers. Anne looked forward to the gifts that would accompany her mother's return. Mrs. McCaffrey eventually circled the globe at least ten times.[3]

Another thing that made Anne's mother quite unusual was what the family called her "feelings" or "the sight." She and her daughter both experienced strong glimpses of the future and were both proved right on many occasions. When the stock market crashed in October 1929, thousands of people lost all their savings. The decade that followed was called the Great Depression, a time of widespread unemployment and poverty. The McCaffreys escaped the worst of it because Anne's mother had one of her "feelings" about the stock market earlier in October and had withdrawn all the money they had invested in it. George McCaffrey had considered this mildly amusing—until the market crashed only days later. If they had left their money in the market, the McCaffreys could have lost their money and their home, as many others did.

Despite her parents' unusual lifestyle and periodic absences, Anne enjoyed a secure childhood. It was a lonely one, though, and she later described herself as "an opinionated . . . impossible . . . brat."[4] The neighborhood children did not want to play with her. In fact, when McCaffrey was at a science fiction convention many years later, talking about her childhood, one of her childhood neighbors stood up and confirmed, "I lived next door to them, and I wouldn't let Anne McCaffrey play in my yard!"[5]

McCaffrey later said that she had given lots of thought to those friendless years. "I wanted to be center-stage all the time. I usually was quick-witted enough to answer all questions in school and annoy the teachers that way—which did me no good with my peer group either. I wasn't a pretty child and I refused to do things I thought were stupid—like playing with dolls, although I do remember enjoying cutting paper-doll clothes. I was never a conformist and consequently would not fall in with any group's ideas of what we should *all* do. I was a . . . tomboy and pre-ferred to climb trees."[6]

Even Anne's brothers did not want to play with her. Her older brother, Hugh (known as "Mac"), either ignored or teased her. Kevin ("Keve") would sometimes stay with her, but he preferred his big brother. So she turned to books and animals for company.

Anne's parents often read to their children. Her father liked the works of Henry Wadsworth Longfellow and Rudyard Kipling. Her mother introduced Anne to early science fiction. Two books, A. Merritt's *The Ship of Ishtar* and Austin Tappan Wright's *Islandia*, were particular favorites of Anne's. She soon tried her own hand at writing and finished her first story, "Flame, Chief of Herd and Track," at age nine. When she imagined her future, though, she saw herself as a singer. She just loved to sing.[7]

With no friends to play with, young Anne sometimes dressed up one of her cats, Thomas, in doll clothes and took him for a stroll in the baby carriage. Then she fell in love with horses. In those days, milk and ice were delivered door-to-door in horse-drawn carts. Anne promised herself that she would own a horse one day. In the meantime, she took riding lessons at the South Orange Arsenal.

When Anne was ten, she went to the Madeleine Mulford Girl Scout Camp and met her first "horse love," an old trotter named Chief.[8] She attended the camp for the next couple of years, and it was there that her life was turned around when she was thirteen. Anne was in the infirmary because of an infected mosquito bite when she overheard several counselors discussing "the McCaffrey brat." A new counselor, Claudia Capps, was going to be taking Anne in hand, and the rest of them were vastly relieved. It was a rude awakening.

Capps was an accomplished horsewoman from Colorado; she quickly became Anne's hero. In an attempt to earn Capps's approval, Anne worked hard on changing her attitude and personality. The transformation lasted a lifetime.

Anne discovered something else at camp that summer: theater. She was chosen to be the stage director for a play based on a Kipling story. It was an especially rainy summer and the campers spent more time indoors than usual. The rain may have put a damper on regular camp activities, but it was a blessing for Anne. She found that she loved being involved with the theater. She would later work onstage and behind the scenes in high school and college, and for many years afterward.

Around that time, Anne's younger brother, Kevin, came down with osteomyelitis, a serious inflammation of the bone and bone marrow. At that time, there was no cure. He went into and out of hospitals as the doctors fought to save his life.

Hugh had been sent to LaSalle Military Academy because, as Anne later described it, "Mother couldn't control him and Dad was away in Albany working on the New York Building Code."[9] Hugh and Anne were not the best of friends, so she did not really miss him. In fact, even when he was gone, he was annoying: He sent his dirty laundry home to be washed, a common practice at the time, and she had to bake "endless quantities" of chocolate chip cookies to be sent back with the clean clothes.[10] Making them from scratch involved pounding hard chunks of chocolate into little chips.

Everything changed on December 7, 1941, when the Japanese bombed the U.S. naval base at Pearl Harbor in Hawaii. War was declared and Anne's father immediately volunteered for active service. He became the quartermaster at the Advanced Air Training Base in Moultrie, Georgia, in 1942. He was responsible for keeping the base well supplied, which was no easy task in wartime. There seemed to be shortages of almost everything. It was not the combat post he had wanted, but he put aside his disappointment, did his best, and "made the Base into the most efficiently run, best-equipped and most sought-after post in the Air Force," according to his daughter.[11]

The family was scattered in the early years of the war. Hugh entered Harvard University in the fall of

1941, following in his father's footsteps. He followed his father again by enlisting in the army in 1943.[12] Anne was a student at Stuart Hall, a boarding school in Virginia. Kevin was in and out of the hospital in New York City, and Anne's mother rented out the house in Montclair. She needed the money to cover Kevin's medical expenses and moved into the city to be closer to him. Sometimes she rented an apartment, and sometimes they stayed with friends. She kept most of her belongings in her old green Buick.[13] McCaffrey, writing about those days, said, "'Home' for Kevin and my mother was often the back" of the car.[14]

Anne started writing poetry, songs, and stories. She had already written three "novels": "Flame, Chief

Anne's parents with her older brother, Hugh, left. In 1943, Anne's father and brother were both in the military.

of Herd and Track," "Eleutheria, the Dancing Slave Girl," and a Western. She wrote some particularly bitter poems about her jealousy of Kevin, who was getting most of their mother's attention, though she knew even then that he needed it the most.[15] She began sending her work out to magazines and collecting rejection slips. She made herself a promise to become a famous author one day.[16]

In 1943, Anne's father was sent to Military Government School in Charlottesville, Virginia, for additional training in administration. Her mother rented a house there, and Kevin entered the University of Virginia Hospital in Charlottesville. He was one of the first patients to be given a new medicine: penicillin. It was not in the pill form often used today. Back then, it was given only as an injection, and the process was painful for Kevin because the fluid was very thick.

When George McCaffrey finally received orders to go overseas, he visited Kevin in the hospital one last time to say good-bye. Anne was deeply shocked by the sight of her usually unemotional father weeping as he left the hospital.[17] The doctors had not been able to make him any promises that Kevin would recover, and he feared he would never see his son alive again. The penicillin did finally prove successful in beating the disease, although Kevin would always bear scars from multiple surgeries and the leg braces he had to wear.

Anne was back at Stuart Hall in May 1943 when she had an experience with "the sight." She woke up from a sound sleep at 3:00 A.M., convinced that something

Anne with Kevin and Hugh in 1943. As children, Anne's brothers teased or ignored her, so she turned to books and animals for company.

was terribly wrong. She could not get back to sleep, and she paced the halls of her dorm until 4:30 A.M. Suddenly the fear was gone and she fell asleep almost immediately. Later that morning, her mother called and they discovered that they had had identical experiences. Her mother was also awake, agitated, from 3:00 to 4:30 A.M. Months afterward, they learned that George McCaffrey had been in mortal danger during their sleepless hours. He was on his way to Algeria, in northwest Africa, when his convoy was attacked by Nazi submarines. While his wife and daughter fretted in the United States, George was sitting in a lifeboat in the middle of the Atlantic Ocean!

George McCaffrey was not without a touch of "the sight" himself. One dark night, the Colonel was being driven to his base in Italy when he suddenly ordered the driver to stop. He got out of the car, walked forward a little, and found that the bridge that had been there was gone. Had they driven even two feet farther, they would have fallen into a gorge and been killed. The replacement bridge was named after him: Ponte del Caffreo.

In the summer of 1943, Anne moved back to New Jersey and lived with family and friends while she completed her senior year of high school in Montclair. She took an accelerated course, starting in the summer and finishing with the fall/winter semester.[18] In February 1944, she received notice that she had been accepted by Radcliffe College, affiliated with Harvard University and considered one of the country's finest women's colleges. Later that year, she moved to Cambridge, Massachusetts, to begin the next chapter of her life.

School Days

When Anne McCaffrey entered Radcliffe in 1944, it was not as common as it is today for women to go to college. The freshman class she joined was small and was chosen from applicants from across the country. McCaffrey's parents were determined that their daughter would advance academically—and that she would excel.

She did both. McCaffrey chose a wide variety of courses. Her studies included cartography (mapmaking), Celtic folk legends, Chinese philosophers, history, U.S. foreign policy, English literature, and Russian. This breadth in subject matter reflected her belief that "a college education teaches you how to find out, absorb, what you don't know."[1] Years later, she would let one of her favorite characters, Robinton, speak up in *The White Dragon* regarding education: "Exchange information, learn to talk sensibly about any subject, learn to express your thoughts, accept new ones, examine them, analyze. Think objectively. Think toward the future."[2]

Everything McCaffrey learned from her courses came into play when she became a writer. When she creates new worlds for her books, she gives them a strong sense of place and often includes maps, thanks to her cartography studies. The Celtic lore came in handy for her books set in early Britain, *Black Horses for the King* and *No One Noticed the Cat*. She quoted the Chinese philosophers in *The Ship Who Searched* and used the Slavonic languages she studied for characters in *The Ship Who Sang* and *To Ride Pegasus*.

The dean at Radcliffe was not sure that McCaffrey was capable of doing the work required for the demanding major she finally chose: Slavonic languages and literature. As it happened, the department head, Samuel Cross, had been a classmate of Anne's father's. Cross told the dean that George McCaffrey's daughter was certain to have the brains necessary for *any* class she took.[3] The dean gave in, reluctantly, and Anne proceeded to prove Cross's prediction to be accurate.

War or no war, Radcliffe students were expected to maintain appearances. A pamphlet printed by the Student Government Association of Radcliffe gave advice on a variety of topics, including how to properly accept an invitation; appropriate clothing on campus ("slacks, shorts, bluejeans are tabu, but ski pants

Invitations
A formal invitation must be answered formally and promptly.

Introductions
One way to preserve poise is to know how to introduce people properly.

Public Appearance
Hats are not needed for Chapel, but should be worn to formal teas. . . . In public . . . slacks, shorts, blue-jeans are tabu. . . . Sunbathing in public . . . is not a Good Idea. . . . And do sit without imitating the octopus.

Private Manners
Neatness is something we all need now and forever.

Here and There
Tea is served every afternoon in the cafeteria.

A student pamphlet, "Public Appearance and Poise at Radcliffe," was filled with rules for college life.

may be worn to classes in sub-zero weather. . . ."); the dangers of accepting blind dates; and the importance of good manners.[4] McCaffrey broke most of those rules, especially the dress code. One rainy day, for example, she took a barefoot stroll down Brattle Street and was caught by the dean of women, who was not amused. McCaffrey shrugged it off; she had only one pair of shoes and did not want to ruin them.[5]

In between writing papers for classes, Anne wrote what she now describes as bad poetry. She also began performing, acting in the theater and on radio. She took part in shows put on by the USO, an organization that provided services and entertainment for American soldiers at home and abroad.[6] She studied voice briefly but could not afford many lessons.

During World War II, Radcliffe students could attend school year-round and graduate early. Anne attended classes for four trimesters in a row. At the end of the fourth trimester, she was told to take off the next two summers to rest. So she did, in her own fashion. Never one to sit still, Anne worked at a variety of jobs. She was a waitress, baby-sitter, cook, and dessert chef. She was at this last job on April 12, 1945, when President Franklin Delano Roosevelt died unexpectedly from a cerebral hemorrhage (bleeding within the brain). "I remember that the two main chefs exchanged glances, turned off the heat on all the stove burners, took off their aprons and went out to tell the clients that the restaurant would be closing as a mark of respect. No one argued. Everyone was weeping."[7] Roosevelt's sudden death was devastating to much of the American public, and it fell to his vice president, Harry S. Truman, to lead the country through to the war's end later that year.

The war affected life at Radcliffe in a variety of ways. As the bulk of America's resources were given over to the war effort, there were widespread short-ages of many supplies. The school's menu became notably dull, and the students all had to take turns serving meals because of a lack of cafeteria workers. Although there were clothing shortages, Anne did not find them much of a bother because she was not especially fashion-conscious.[8]

What did bother her at first was the lackluster social life. Radcliffe is affiliated with Harvard, but most of the men on campus were not, in McCaffrey's opinion, her type at all. She was glad when soldiers returning from the war livened things up.

While McCaffrey was at Radcliffe, her family was spread out over the globe. Her mother and Kevin had moved back to the house in Montclair. Hugh was in the army. He had been shipped out to the Pacific but was recalled and sent to Fort Benning, Georgia, for officer training. George McCaffrey was in England, where he had arrived just before Germany began launching its terrifying "buzz bombs"—rocket-propelled bombs that made a terrible buzzing sound as they approached their targets—across the English Channel.

When the fall of 1945 rolled around, Kevin entered Harvard. Hugh returned to the university just one semester later and the brothers roomed together. There was no washing machine in their dorm, but there was in Anne's, so she wound up lugging their laundry back and forth between Radcliffe and

Harvard. Contrary to any expectations she might have had, having brothers at Harvard did not do much for her social life either. "Mac didn't think I was pretty enough to introduce to his friends and Keve was positive that none of his friends were good enough for his sister, so they were no help at all."[9]

Still, the brothers did come in handy when one of their dormmates made rude comments about Anne after a less than pleasant date. He earned himself an impressive black eye, and Anne's good reputation was promptly restored.[10]

Back in New Jersey, Anne's mother had found work that suited her perfectly. She became very successful as a real-estate agent. George McCaffrey made it home in 1947, just in time to see his daughter graduate *cum laude*—with honors—from Radcliffe.

Off to Work

It was 1948. The war had been over for three years. The United States was entering a period of great prosperity, and Anne McCaffrey needed a job.

Off she went to New York City, where she worked as a secretary/translator for World Trade Intelligence for three months. She moved on to a position as a secretary for a manufacturing company. Her boss, Willie Freeman, introduced her to the joys of sailing.[1] Her knowledge of sailing and ships later surfaced in several of her books.

That was not enough to keep McCaffrey there, though. Onward, then, to a job as a copywriter and graphic designer for Liberty Music Shops. She wrote descriptions of their merchandise and helped to create eye-catching advertisements. McCaffrey enjoyed this work and took great pleasure in living across the street from Carnegie Hall, the world-famous concert hall. She spent two years working at Liberty, then took a job as a copywriter and secretary at Helena Rubenstein, the cosmetics firm.[2]

In 1949, McCaffrey met H. Wright Johnson. He was a graduate of Princeton University and a reporter for *Women's Wear Daily*, a newspaper for people in the clothing industry. Introduced by mutual friends, they found they had many interests in common—opera, ballet, and music among them—and began dating. They married on January 14, 1950, and moved into an apartment on East Forty-eighth Street, an area later taken over as part of the grounds for the United Nations. Years later, McCaffrey described their first home as "three small rooms and plenty of cockroaches."[3] After a few months, they moved uptown to Fifty-seventh Street. The new apartment was large, but it got very little light and was fairly gloomy.

It was there that McCaffrey began reading contemporary science fiction novels. She was stuck at home with a nasty case of bronchitis. One day she was desperate for something to read and picked up some science fiction novels that the previous tenants had left behind. She was hooked. Her husband was appalled by her taste in literature, but she kept on reading. Soon she began writing, too. Then she began to wonder—what was she to do with her stories?

As it happened, McCaffrey's former roommate, Betty Wragge, knew an editor at Ziff-Davis, a publishing company that owned two science fiction magazines,

After college, McCaffrey moved to New York City. There she began reading—and writing—science fiction.

Fantastic and *Amazing*. Anne began sending her work to this editor, Lila Schafer. Although McCaffrey never did get a story into either magazine, she received a great deal of instruction and constructive criticism. She later said that she might never have gotten anything published at all were it not for Lila Schafer's timely help.[4]

In late 1951, McCaffrey became pregnant. She and Johnson moved to New Jersey, where they rented an apartment in a house her mother owned in Upper Montclair. At the time, both her parents were in Japan, where the Colonel was hard at work helping the Japanese government revise the country's tax system.[5]

As McCaffrey's pregnancy progressed, physical problems arose. She finally quit her office job in 1952 on the advice of her doctor. Fortunately, Alexander Anthony Johnson, called Alec, was perfectly healthy when he was born on August 29. McCaffrey kept up her writing, usually during Alec's naps.[6] Out went the stories, back came the rejection slips. At last, in 1953, McCaffrey received an acceptance letter and a check for $100. She had made her first sale, to Sam Moskowitz at *Science Fiction Plus*. She was ecstatic.

McCaffrey was, in some ways, revolutionary for the times. Even as the mother of a young child, she continued to work, although it was part-time and from her home. She was writing science fiction, an unusual genre for a woman. In the early 1950s, married women like McCaffrey were expected to stay home with the children and keep house. It did not matter if they were college graduates or had good jobs prior to their marriages. Men were supposed to be the sole wage earners, and some found it embarrassing to have wives who worked. They thought it reflected poorly on their ability to provide for their families.

McCaffrey's husband was immensely displeased with her writing, but mostly because he thought of science fiction as trash. When Anne's first published story, "Freedom of the Race," ran in the October 1953 issue of *Science Fiction Plus*, it rated an article in their local paper, the *Montclair Times*. The reporter noted: "Being a Princeton man, Mr. Johnson takes a somewhat dim view of his wife's flights into outer space. He

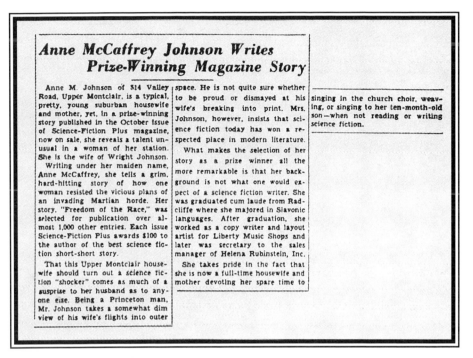

Anne McCaffrey Johnson Writes Prize-Winning Magazine Story

Anne M. Johnson of 514 Valley Road, Upper Montclair, is a typical, pretty, young suburban housewife and mother, yet, in a prize-winning story published in the October issue of Science-Fiction Plus magazine, now on sale, she reveals a talent unusual in a woman of her station. She is the wife of Wright Johnson.

Writing under her maiden name, Anne McCaffrey, she tells a grim, hard-hitting story of how one woman resisted the vicious plans of an invading Martian horde. Her story, "Freedom of the Race," was selected for publication over almost 1,000 other entries. Each issue Science-Fiction Plus awards $100 to the author of the best science fiction short-short story.

That this Upper Montclair housewife should turn out a science fiction "shocker" comes as much of a surprise to her husband as to anyone else. Being a Princeton man, Mr. Johnson takes a somewhat dim view of his wife's flights into outer space. He is not quite sure whether to be proud or dismayed at his wife's breaking into print. Mrs. Johnson, however, insists that science fiction today has won a respected place in modern literature.

What makes the selection of her story as a prize winner all the more remarkable is that her background is not what one would expect of a science fiction writer. She was graduated cum laude from Radcliffe where she majored in Slavonic languages. After graduation, she worked as a copy writer and layout artist for Liberty Music Shops and later was secretary to the sales manager of Helena Rubinstein, Inc.

She takes pride in the fact that she is now a full-time housewife and mother devoting her spare time to singing in the church choir, weaving, or singing to her ten-month-old son—when not reading or writing science fiction.

On August 13, 1953, The Montclair Times *reported the success of local writer Anne McCaffrey.*

is not quite sure whether to be proud or dismayed at his wife's breaking into print."[7] Johnson never did change his mind about science fiction, and many years later he told one of McCaffrey's editors, Judy-Lynn Del Rey, that his name was not to be mentioned in any publicity releases about his wife.[8] For her author's byline, Anne has always used the name McCaffrey, not Johnson.

McCaffrey's parents returned to the United States in 1953. During a routine medical checkup, her father was found to have tuberculosis, a serious disease that usually affects the lungs. He was sent to the Castle

Point Veterans Hospital in New York. As she had when he was in danger in World War II, McCaffrey had a flash of "the sight" and knew in her heart that her father's illness would prove fatal. On the morning of January 25, 1954, George Herbert McCaffrey died.

Anne was devastated. After her father's death, the sight of a flag-draped coffin or the sound of taps—the bugle call blown at night and at military funerals—was more than enough to move her to tears. Years later, in the preface to her 1969 novel *The Ship Who Sang*, she described the book as "an unconscious attempt to ease my grief over the death of my father, the Colonel."[9]

Still, in 1954 she had a child and a husband to care for, and more stories to write, so life went on. Her second son, Todd, was born on April 27, 1956. With two young children in the house, McCaffrey's life was full. Not full enough, however. There was an unsuccessful revolution against the Communist regime in Hungary that year, and many people fled the country. When Americans living on the East Coast were asked to take in refugees, McCaffrey and Johnson volunteered. Sixteen-year-old Josef Kaldi, who swam the Danube River to reach freedom in Austria, came to live with them. He stayed with their family until he enlisted in the United States Army in 1962.[10]

It took almost that long for McCaffrey to sell another story.

On the Move

Six years is a long time to go without the encouragement provided by success. McCaffrey, though, just kept writing and sending out stories—in between changing diapers, doing laundry, making dinner, and keeping house.

In 1957, she sent a love story about parapsychics to *Fantasy and Science Fiction* magazine. It was tossed into what publishers call the "slush pile"—all the material sent in by writers hoping to be published. Another writer, Algis Budrys, was working there at the time, and the story caught his eye. He showed it to editor Bob Mills, and McCaffrey had her second sale.[1] This novella, *The Lady in the Tower*, was published in 1959. McCaffrey was back in print.

Her life was moving in other directions as well.

Johnson was working for Du Pont, a large chemical corporation, and was transferred to Wilmington, Delaware, in August 1958. There they bought Anne's favorite house, a Cape Cod–style cottage with four bedrooms, lots of space, and a big yard.[2]

It proved to be a crucial move for McCaffrey, for it was in Wilmington that she returned to work in music and theater. She started with the church choir, in which Johnson also sang. Next she ventured into local amateur theatrical troupes, in particular the Lancaster Opera Company. There she studied stage direction with Frederic H. Robinson, who became the model for a beloved McCaffrey character. Her readers will recognize him as Robinton, the Masterharper of Pern, who is described as a master musician, diplomat, and charmer. He appeared in the first of the Pern books, *Dragonflight*, and, McCaffrey says, "horned into ten of the books. There's no way I can keep him out."[3]

McCaffrey was enjoying her return to the stage. She loved to sing and she had a dramatic flair. She also had a three-and-a-half-octave range, which meant she could easily handle both alto and soprano parts, giving her an advantage over many other singers. Still, some of her high notes were "rather ear-piercing," she said later.[4] Robinson suggested that she concentrate more on stage direction than on performing, and she did just that.

She also took a big step for herself as a writer. Pregnant with her third child (Georgeanne—"Gigi"—born on August 27, 1959), McCaffrey went to Milford, Pennsylvania, to attend her first Science Fiction

In Wilmington, Delaware, McCaffrey, shown here with her son Todd, was delighted to return to the stage, both performing and directing local theater.

Writers' Conference. The conference was a gathering of professional writers of science fiction and fantasy, and attendance was by invitation only. McCaffrey was thrilled to have been invited. She met other writers who would go on to become leading lights in science fiction—Robert Silverberg, Judith Merril, Harlan Ellison, Kate Wilhelm, and James Blish among them. For one intense week, the attendees read one another's work and offered their comments. Although it was difficult, she said, to listen as her stories were "ripped into tiny shreds" by other writers, the criticism, support, and encouragement McCaffrey received were vital to her development as a writer.[5]

McCaffrey met another key to her career at the Milford conference: Virginia Kidd. Four years later, Kidd decided to go into business as an agent for science fiction writers. McCaffrey became one of her first clients. Equipped with in-depth knowledge of the science fiction genre and fine-tuned skills as a copy editor and writer, Kidd was a tremendous influence on McCaffrey, helping with sentence structure and grammar in early drafts of her work. When McCaffrey sent her the first version of *Dragonquest*, Kidd told her to burn it and start over. She did.[6] Bit by bit, things were falling into place for McCaffrey as a writer.

Then, in 1963, the whole family moved to Düsseldorf, West Germany, for several months. Johnson had been chosen to form a German promotion and publicity bureau for Du Pont. Alec and Todd were enrolled in a local elementary school, and all three children learned quite a bit of German—even three-year-old Gigi.

Both McCaffrey and Johnson were able to indulge their love of music in Düsseldorf, often attending the Deutsche Oper am Rhein and meeting the visiting American singers. They both studied voice with a teacher Anne credits with worsening a flaw in her voice. Still, that training was of great value to McCaffrey when she returned to Wilmington. In December 1963, she was invited to direct the American premiere of Carl Orff's opera *Ludus de Nato Infante Mirificus*, which was sung in German. In addition to her chores as stage director, McCaffrey sang in the chorus and had a solo part as a witch.

At this point in her life, McCaffrey had three little

ones ranging in age from four to eleven, a large house to manage, and an ongoing involvement in musical theater. It was certainly enough to fill the day and then some. But she was also busy making up stories, and she plunged back into her writing.

In 1964, she hired a baby-sitter to watch the children for three hours a day, during which time she would write. And write she did, turning out more Helva *(The Ship Who Sang)* stories and two fledgling novels. One of these would later become *Restoree*, her first published novel. It was bought by Betty Ballantine, of Ballantine Books, in 1966 and published in 1967.

Restoree introduces a strong, independent-minded

This is Anne McCaffrey's favorite photo of her daughter, Gigi, with Silky Blackington the cat.

female character. McCaffrey had no patience with the women who populated the science fiction stories of the time. They were usually beautiful, a trifle stupid, and utterly helpless; they always needed to be rescued from someone or something. McCaffrey's heroine, Sara, was different. Kidnapped by aliens, she used her own wits to regain her freedom and in the process saved an entire planet. McCaffrey wrote it as a spoof of the helpless-female books, a gleeful turning of the tables, but many reviewers missed the point entirely. The book received mixed reviews.

In 1965, the family moved once more. Du Pont had transferred Johnson yet again, this time to New York. His assistant, Jack Isbell, was transferred too. To make living in the New York City area affordable, the families moved into an enormous house in Sea Cliff, on Long Island. It was quite a scene: one house, three stories, nine bedrooms, ten bathrooms, four adults, five children, many cats, and one dog. The arrangement worked remarkably well for five years.

In 1970, writer David Gerrold visited and described the house as "a masterpiece of gothic horror . . . a location appropriately exotic enough for Anne McCaffrey." He added that the house was "in a state of constant uproar . . . a polite way of saying Anne doesn't keep house too good. But when you've spent a whole day saving the solar system, exploring the Galaxy, and re-aligning the Universe, not to mention beating off the Alien Invasion . . . who has time to do the dishes?"[7]

Not McCaffrey. She had some writing to do.

Up in the Air

By 1966, the children were in school during the day, and McCaffrey had more time for science fiction. She became the secretary/treasurer of Science Fiction Writers of America (SFWA), a post she held until 1970. And now McCaffrey could concentrate more on her writing. She worked in a small room on the first floor, at the back of the house. It was crammed full of books, file cabinets, a typewriter, and even a bed. One day in May, she went to her office, determined to start a new short story, and dreamed up Pern.

"I sat down . . . to think up new critters for a story—and came up with dragons, their symbiotic partners, and Pern. I spent all day, until the kids got home from school, setting out the parameters of the story, as well as the world that needed the special abilities of the dragons I envisaged as Pern's renewable air-defense system. Mind you, I cheated a bit: I used an Earth-type planet."[1]

Why dragons? This is a question McCaffrey is asked on a regular basis. She says, "Dragons had had very bad press. When I found myself wanting to use an alien 'critter' in my writing, I remembered that. What I did differently was to put dragons on an equal footing with humans." She also made them telepathic creatures—able to communicate with humans by thought—who bonded for life with just one person, their rider. The dragons were an immediate hit with

When many people think of Anne McCaffrey, they think of dragons. In 1988, McCaffrey was asked to dedicate a dragon statue by Loren McLean in her friend David Willis's garden.

readers of all ages. After all, says McCaffrey, "Wouldn't *you* like to have a forty-foot telepathic dragon for your best friend?"[2]

Within four years of moving to Sea Cliff, McCaffrey was writing at a tremendous pace. She published eight short stories, including four of her Brainship tales: "The Ship Who Mourned," "The Ship Who Killed," "Dramatic Mission," and "The Ship Who Disappeared." The heroine, Helva, is a woman who is part of a spaceship; she is its brain and it houses her body, which would not survive without total life-support equipment. Far from feeling imprisoned, she feels a little sorry for "soft shell" humans who have so little power and cannot fly through the galaxy at will.

Three of the other four stories deal with people who have psychic talents: "A Meeting of Minds," "Apple," and "A Womanly Talent" explore the possibilities of telepathy, telekinesis (the ability to move objects with mental power), and teleportation (the ability to transport objects from one location to another instantly, again with mental power). There is quite a bit of technology involved in the stories—machines are used to boost and measure the psychics' gifts—but the hardware is a backdrop for the characters and not the other way around. People always come first with McCaffrey.

The last story published in this period, "The Weather on Welladay," was a combination of science fiction and mystery, with a reminder that humans must be mindful and protective of the environment and all who share it. Again there was plenty of technology, but it was all used to support the story and the characters.

During those same four years, McCaffrey also wrote two novellas set on Pern—*Weyr Search* and *Dragonrider*—and finished four novels. The novels were *Restoree*, the take-off on old-fashioned science fiction; *Dragonflight*, the first Pern book; *Dragonquest*, its sequel; and *Decision at Doona*. The hero of the Doona book is a young, bright, stubborn boy named Todd, and, yes, he is modeled after Anne's son. The book is dedicated "To Todd Johnson—of course!"

With the exception of *Decision at Doona*, all of these books center on strong-minded, independent women. McCaffrey did not, however, make the male characters take on the helpless-victim role that female characters often played in other writers' stories. The men and boys in her books are not cardboard cutouts; they come in all sizes and strengths. And McCaffrey creates just as many male heroes as she does male villains.

McCaffrey also began putting young people into her work, and she forever endeared herself to count-less readers by making those characters as real as possible. They have minds of their own, they make mistakes and have to deal with the consequences, they have tempers and active senses of humor. Some of them have had to break free of people or places in order to follow their dreams. McCaffrey's fictional children are not perfect, nor are they living perfect lives, and readers root for them from page one.

McCaffrey began to receive writing awards. In 1968, she learned that she had been nominated for

By 1969, Anne McCaffrey was becoming known for her strong, independent heroines. Here she talks with fellow writers Gordie Dickson and Hal Clement at the Worldcon science fiction convention in St. Louis, Missouri.

the Hugo Award for Best Novella for *Weyr Search* and a Nebula Award from the Science Fiction Writers of America for Best Novella for *Dragonrider*.

Shortly before the Hugo ceremony, she took a vacation to England and Ireland with a favorite relative, her Aunt Gladys. They had a great time together, and Anne fell in love with Ireland. It was peaceful, beautiful, and she felt at home almost immediately. They went to a horse show in Dublin and toured the southern counties. "It was just a gorgeous place to be," said McCaffrey. "I cried when the airplane took off from Limerick."[3] She made it back to the United

States just in time to go to Oakland, California, where she became the first woman to win the Hugo Award.[4]

When she arrived in Oakland, college students from the nearby University of California, Berkeley, were rioting to protest the war in Vietnam. The scent of tear gas was in the air as the demonstrators battled with troops from the National Guard. It was quite a contrast to the serene, friendly Ireland she had just left. The United States was deeply divided over the war. Those who supported it saw the protesters as traitors to their country. The peace activists felt equally strongly that the war was wrong and that too many people were dying without good cause. Many families were split by bitter political arguments. In the Johnson household, though, the discussions bore extra heat: Alec was eligible to be drafted into the military.

At the time, many young men chose to evade the draft by moving to Canada. McCaffrey's husband was determined that Alec would take that route rather than go into the army. McCaffrey, the daughter and sister of military men, would have preferred that he serve his country. Still, she felt that Alec would have to live with that decision forever and that he—not his parents—should be the one to make it. Alec was completely opposed to the war and had decided that he would go to Canada if necessary.[5] As it turned out, Alec was not drafted.

Meanwhile, McCaffrey and Johnson's marriage was beginning to fall apart. Johnson still did not approve of science fiction. He urged Anne to switch to something more conventionally literate, but she refused to do so. At the time, Johnson was not very happy at work. He had an artistic nature and was working for a very rigid company. It was a bad fit in many ways and his frustrations carried over into his home life. Todd later wrote that "bitter arguments broke out across the dinner table. Wright would retire early to his room to play classical music and drink wine, to the relief of the rest of the family."[6] His children did not like his punishments. "Wright's ideas of discipline were typical for a child of the Depression—a belt, a shoe, a cane reed . . . ," recalled Todd.[7]

Johnson began to spend more time away from home. Sometimes he traveled to Europe for three weeks at a time. On his return, he would often argue with McCaffrey over family decisions she had made in his absence. McCaffrey told Johnson that he had to stop drinking, but he did not.[8] He moved to an apartment in New York City, saying that commuting from Long Island was too tiring. McCaffrey spoke to a lawyer about getting a divorce in October 1969.

The Isbells told McCaffrey that she and the children would have to leave their shared house at the end of the school year. Johnson recommended that they move to Princeton, New Jersey, known for excellent schools. McCaffrey told him instead that she was divorcing him and taking the children to Ireland. After months of legal battles, McCaffrey flew to Mexico in 1970 and got a divorce. When she returned, she cleared her family's belongings out of the Sea Cliff house.

Then McCaffrey told Gigi and Todd that they would be moving to Ireland. Alec was about to begin college, so he was staying in the United States. At first, Gigi was excited by the adventure her mother made it out to be. When she realized that she would be leaving her friends behind, she went to her mother in tears. Once McCaffrey reassured her that she would make new friends in Ireland, Gigi was ready to go. Todd, however, was terribly upset by the divorce and the move. He later said, "fourteen's a delicate age."[9]

Toward the end of the summer, McCaffrey took Gigi and Todd to Toronto. She and writer Isaac Asimov were the guests of honor at a science fiction convention there. On August 25, 1970, the family boarded a plane in Toronto, on their way to the greener pastures of Ireland.

Happy Landings

It was foggy in Dublin. So foggy, in fact, that the plane was held at Shannon Airport while the airline waited for the weather to clear. After several hours, it became obvious that the fog was not going to budge. The passengers were rounded up and bused to Shannon's train station. Then off they went to Dublin. From there it was a short ride to Dun Laoghaire, where McCaffrey and the children had hotel rooms waiting.

McCaffrey's mother came over a week later to help the family hunt for a house to rent. They finally found one in Mount Merrion, a few miles from the school the children would be attending. The house had four bedrooms and a walled garden. Mrs. McCaffrey returned home, packed, put some things in storage, and came back to Ireland to live with her daughter and grandchildren.

Anne McCaffrey had chosen to move to Ireland for several reasons: her Irish ancestry, the good schools, the sheer distance it would put between her and her ex-husband, and Ireland's recently passed Haughey's Artists Exemption Act. This law exempted writers from paying taxes on their earnings, and it provided McCaffrey with the extra financial relief she needed.

Gigi called the first years in Ireland "the pancake years" because they ate lots of cheap homemade pancakes.[1] Still, McCaffrey managed to pay for horseback riding lessons for the children. Gigi turned out to be just as crazy about horses as her mother. Todd was not quite as enthusiastic, but he quickly became a good rider. They all rode whenever they could.

In February 1971, McCaffrey met a horse who was to be a part of her life for the next ten years, Mr. Ed. When she arrived at Iris Kellett's stables on Mespil Road, it was love at first ride. McCaffrey bought the huge dapple-gray horse in May and paid for him in installments over the next year.

McCaffrey got more than a horse out of that visit. She referred to Iris Kellett as a superb rider in her 1987 book *The Lady* and used "Mespil" years later as the name of a major character in her Planet Pirates/Dinosaur Planet books. In fact, her readers can find quite a number of her interplanetary place names on a good map of Ireland.

When she was not riding and working at a stable to help pay for Mr. Ed's stabling, Anne McCaffrey was writing. Three novels were published that year,

McCaffrey rides one of her favorite horses, Mr. Ed—also often called "Horseface."

including *Dragonquest*, the sequel to *Dragonflight*. The other two were romances that drew heavily on her own background: *The Mark of Merlin* features military men and a German shepherd modeled on a dog she once owned, and *Ring of Fear* takes place in the horse world. Both romances were well received by the critics and the public, and they sold well.[2]

McCaffrey also edited a collection of science fiction and fantasy entitled *Alchemy and Academe* and sold several short stories. One of them, "The Thorns of Barevi," would be revisited and developed into the Catteni series of books more than twenty years later: *Freedom's Landing*, *Freedom's Choice*, and *Freedom's*

Challenge. McCaffrey went through reams of paper and a box of typewriter ribbons, and bit by bit the family finances began to improve. McCaffrey was selling new stories and receiving royalty payments for the books already in print.

Meanwhile, Gigi and Todd were settling into life in Ireland. Gigi went off in search of friends as soon as they moved into their new house. A neighbor told her where a girl her age lived, so she walked right up to the door, knocked, and announced that she had come to make friends with Anne Kelly. And so she did![3] Todd had a harder time. He eventually made friends with other foreigners, boys from England and Denmark. He missed living in the United States, though.

Back in the United States, Alec was struggling with his freshman year of college. He finally left Stony Brook College, in New York, and came to Ireland in 1972. Although Anne McCaffrey had some projects in the works, all of 1972 went by without any new books hitting the stores, and money was tight. The family was living in Dundrum then, renting a 220-year-old Georgian mansion, the Meadowbrook. It was a large, two-story stone house with stables and a bit of land for Mr. Ed. Alec worked as a cook on a fishing boat, then hunted rabbits on the Blaskett Islands off the southwest coast of Ireland. Not cut out for a career as a hunter, Alec took a job working for a community group called Simon-Ireland that helped the poor. He returned to the United States in 1973, moving to Boston.

Anne McCaffrey picked up her writing pace in 1973. She concentrated mostly on short stories, many of which were published in collections edited by science fiction anthologist Roger Elwood. She also edited *Cooking Out of This World*, a book of recipes donated by science fiction writers. Betty Ballantine had cooked up the idea as a way to add to McCaffrey's "going-away fund" back in 1970. The recipes ranged from Café Ellison Diabolique, from her diabolical and devoted friend Harlan Ellison, to McCaffrey's own Irish potato pancakes.[4]

Things were going fairly smoothly as the summer of 1974 came around. They were in yet another rented house, this one in Shanganagh Vale. Alec had found a summer job for Todd in Boston. Gigi was in Bordeaux, France, vacationing with a friend's family.

Then McCaffrey's mother had a sudden, terrible stroke in June. Although her mother was unable to communicate, McCaffrey knew that she was aware of her surroundings and of her predicament. McCaffrey would sit at her mother's bedside, talking about the day's goings-on and holding her hand. When she was no longer able to bear seeing her mother in that condition, she would flee the room to weep in the hall.[5] In July, her mother suffered a second major stroke and died. It was not until the following year, 1975, that Anne was able to honor her mother's wishes and bring her ashes back to the United States to be placed in her husband's grave in Boston.

McCaffrey had come to Boston as the guest of honor at a science fiction convention, the Boskone XV. There she received the E. E. "Doc" Smith Lensman Award, given to those who were considered to be particularly good storytellers in the Doc Smith tradition. "Doc Smith wrote walloping good adventure yarns, lightly based on some sort of scientific extrapolation," says McCaffrey.[6] It was the first of many trips she made to the United States for science fiction conventions and lecture tours.

That year she wrote the stories that later blossomed into the Crystal Singer series. McCaffrey named her main character after a chance conversation. "Someone asked me if I liked the name Killashandra and I said yes very much. They told me it was a [brand] name for butter and I said it was wasted for butter! That night when I got home I wrote the first page and a half of *Crystal Singer* and I went back to it later."[7]

McCaffrey drew heavily on her own experiences as a singer to create yet another strong, independent heroine. Killashandra studies hard, aiming for the top of her profession, only to be told to give up her dreams because her voice is flawed. When McCaffrey was in much the same position some years earlier, she left the stage—Killashandra leaves the planet! McCaffrey's tales of Killashandra were chosen for three successive anthologies compiled by Roger Elwood.

She made a quick switch to nonfiction writing with "Hitch Your Dragon to a Star: Romance and Glamour in Science Fiction." It appeared in a collection of essays entitled *Science Fiction, Today & Tomorrow*. In her essay, McCaffrey gleefully relates the history of women in science fiction, both as characters in stories and as writers.

One writer later put forward the theory that Anne

does not like men, because she writes about so many strong women and has never remarried. She is both amused and a little appalled by the idea. She points out that there are intelligent, strong, sensitive, and attractive men in every book she has written. As for remarrying, she chose to devote her time to earning a living for herself and her children and it was a full-time occupation.[8]

Full-time indeed. In 1975, McCaffrey wrote two more books, *The Kilternan Legacy* and *A Time When*, and a short story, "Killashandra—Coda and Finale." *The Kilternan Legacy* is the tale of a newly divorced American woman who goes to Ireland with her two children to see property left to her by an aunt she barely knew. McCaffrey says that although it does bear some resemblance to her own story, parts of it were modeled on the experiences of one of her friends.[9] *A Time When*, another Pern tale, later became part of *The White Dragon*. The short story about Killashandra was published in yet another Roger Elwood anthology and then later incorporated into *Crystal Singer*. Since her arrival in Ireland, McCaffrey had completed five novels and one short story collection, published more than a dozen short stories, and edited two books.

The work was going well, but trouble loomed at home. Gigi was diagnosed with Crohn's disease, an incurable inflammation of the small intestines. Both mother and daughter were badly shaken.[10]

A year or so earlier, McCaffrey had been asked to write a book for teenagers. It took a while for her to get it done to her satisfaction, but in 1976 she began her

Harper Hall series. Bantam Books bought *Dragonsong*, which came out that year, and *Dragonsinger*, which was published in 1977. They were tremendous hits.

The heroine of both books is a young woman named Menolly. She is a gifted musician who lives in a remote seaside location on Pern, the planet McCaffrey created in *Dragonflight*. Her parents do not want her to waste her time on music when there is work to be done. In their society, women cannot be harpers (Pern's professional musicians who also serve as historians and teachers). Menolly finally runs away from home and winds up exactly where she belongs: in the Harper Hall. Along the way she overcomes many difficulties and finds support from other young people, making the first true friends of her life. Menolly also bonds with nine fire lizards—the tiny dragons that are the ancestors of the large ones developed by Pern's original colonists. Her adventures and determination to be true to herself make both books real page-turners. Readers *must* know what happens next! That is possibly McCaffrey's greatest gift: She creates characters that readers can identify with and places them in well-plotted, captivating stories.

McCaffrey begins writing her stories with a scene, and with characters in conflict. "I do not plan a novel. I take a situation and people logically involved in that situation."[11] She never outlines her stories in advance. Instead, the plot grows naturally as she types. A novel "'tells' itself one way, bogs down hopelessly if I try to 'force' it another . . . ," she says.[12] She tunes in to her own reactions. If she cannot decide where the story should go next, or if she is getting bored with the tale, she knows it is time for a new twist of plot. "I put in a new character or switch to a new theme and then go back and work it all in," she explains.[13]

McCaffrey devotes many hours to her work, starting early in the morning and often sitting at the keyboard up to twelve hours a day. She revises and rewrites, "sometimes a whole 'nother novel's worth," she says.[14] And she does not write at night, reserving evening hours for copyediting and for thinking over what she has written so far.

In 1976, McCaffrey took some time off from writing to pack; it was time to move again. The house she had been renting was literally beginning to fall apart. She realized, to her delight, that her dragons had earned her enough money to buy a house. She found one with room for both people and horses and promptly dubbed it Dragonhold.

It was at Dragonhold that she realized an old dream: living with horses. Ever since she was a little girl, McCaffrey had promised herself that she would have horses of her own someday. Now she set out to give Mr. Ed some company in the stable. For Gigi, she bought a gray horse called Ben. Then she asked her friend and fellow horsewoman Jan Regan to come live at Dragonhold and help manage her house and a horse-breeding operation. Anne worried that she might run out of ideas for books and wanted a second source of income.

That was more than forty books ago, and McCaffrey has not had to fall back on her horses for income yet.

Readers can identify with McCaffrey's characters, and they love the twists and turns of her plots. Here, McCaffrey autographs books for her fans.

Get Off the Unicorn, a short-story collection featuring characters with parapsychic abilities, was published in 1977. It included a Pern tale titled "The Smallest Dragonboy." The hero is named K'van as a tribute to Anne's brother Kevin, who had never cried or complained through years of treatments and hospitalizations. It is her most often reprinted story.[15]

When the next Pern book, *The White Dragon*, came out in 1978, it sold enough copies to make *The New York Times* best-seller list. It was the first science fiction hardcover book ever to do so, a distinction of which McCaffrey is very proud.

Another Pern book, *The Dragonriders of Pern*, was released in 1978. It consisted of all three Pern books— *Dragonflight*, *Dragonquest*, and *The White Dragon*—in one edition. That year McCaffrey also published the first book in a new series, *Dinosaur Planet*. In this series, a group of colonists is marooned on a distant world on which there are dinosaurs. McCaffrey was on a roll.

McCaffrey's publisher, Del Rey, decided to send her on a promotional tour in the spring of 1979. She was scheduled to visit twenty-two cities in thirty-two days. McCaffrey was so pleased to be asked to tour that she never thought twice about accepting the itinerary. She had plenty of time to regret her decision while she traveled, though. It took a long time to recover from the physical exhaustion of that coast-to-coast trip.

But it did not stop her from writing.

At Home and on the Road

By 1980, McCaffrey had a home of her own with grounds inhabited by horses, dogs, and cats. All of her children were doing well. Ballantine, her publisher, was keeping her books on the bookstore shelves and the hits just kept coming.

Until they stopped.

McCaffrey was still recuperating from her long book tour and had her hands full with developing her horse business. She did not have much energy left for writing. She finally consulted a psychiatrist for help with the exhaustion and a bout of insomnia. He prescribed a medication that made things worse. McCaffrey felt completely disconnected from her imagination. She asked a friend who worked for a pharmaceutical firm to get more information on the

McCaffrey jokes with Betty Ballantine, her publisher, as Silkie the dog sniffs nearby.

medicine. When he called the manufacturer, he was asked if he was calling about a woman who had died while taking the same drug.

That was enough for McCaffrey, and she threw away the rest of the prescription. She decided she would simply fight through her fatigue and depression by herself. She found it almost impossible to concentrate, even to read. Every night, though, she would make it through a few pages of Robert Silverberg's book *Lord Valentine's Castle*. She credits the book with helping save her sanity. Also, Alec was home for a visit. He was taking a break from classes at the University of Massachusetts (where he had met his future wife, Kate). McCaffrey found her son's company to be a great help.[1]

In the spring of 1980, McCaffrey went to Kansas City for a science fiction convention called the Fool's Con. There she collected two more writing awards, called Balrogs. They were given to her for *Dragondrums*, the third book in the Harper Hall series, and for her entire body of work. The awards were heavy, but she lugged them home. They look "like ugly bats with wings spread," she says, and they now sit atop some bookcases, smiling ominously down at visitors.[2] Later that year, McCaffrey went to Australia on a promotional tour, and Gigi went along.

The early eighties were given over mostly to book tours and work on the Dragonhold Stables. It had been one of McCaffrey's daily pleasures to step out the kitchen door, bellow "Horseface!" and watch Mr. Ed canter over to her. But arthritis had been slowing Mr. Ed down for months, and he was in constant pain. Even walking became difficult for him. In September 1981, McCaffrey had to have Mr. Ed euthanized. It was an awful blow, and she wept bitterly as she bade her dear friend farewell. Late that night the phone rang. It was Alec calling from the United States to announce the arrival of McCaffrey's first grandchild, Eliza Oriana Johnson. The balancing of death with birth became the basis for the last two chapters of McCaffrey's *Moreta: Dragonlady of Pern.*

By spring of 1982, the reputation of Dragonhold Stables was on the rise, thanks in part to the successful performance of a particularly talented horse, Jack, in several horse shows. McCaffrey's storytelling knack was back, too, and toward the end of the year she polished off two more books, *Moreta* and *The Coelura*, both published in 1983. *Moreta* is the tale of a courageous, independent woman who plays a crucial role in helping to fight a deadly plague on Pern. McCaffrey backtracked in time to create some of Pern's history, setting *Moreta* in an earlier time period than her first Pern book, *Dragonflight.*

The worlds and society McCaffrey created for *The Coelura* were to serve as the basis for *Nimisha's Ship*, which would be published sixteen years later, in 1999, and promptly become a best-seller. Set in the future, in a technologically advanced culture, both books feature a rigid society in which extremely wealthy families have tremendous power and influence. The heroines break society's rules and make contributions to their worlds that would have been impossible had they simply gone along with what they were expected to do and be.

Crystal Singer, the book she had made out of the Killashandra stories, was published in 1982. In 1983, Mayfair Games brought out a board game called *Dragonriders of Pern*. The company hired an illustrator named Robin Wood for the project. Illustrator and author worked together closely, so Wood could portray the characters McCaffrey saw so clearly in her mind's eye. McCaffrey was delighted with the results.[3]

In 1983, McCaffrey was still hard at work making a success of the horse business, but she also found time to write two more books, *Dinosaur Planet Survivors* and *A Stitch in Snow*. *Stitch* was not science fiction and was inspired by an actual event.

The book is about a romance that starts when a traveling author meets a man in the Denver, Colorado, airport. The author is knitting an Aran sweater (McCaffrey excels at this complicated style of knitting, which originated in Ireland). When the author drops a ball of yarn, a handsome man retrieves it for her. Up to that point, it is all true. McCaffrey was indeed sitting in the airport in Denver, knitting away, when she dropped a ball of yarn and a handsome man picked it up. There the similarity ends, however. In reality, they proceeded to their flights and never saw each other again. But McCaffrey spun this chance encounter into a book.[4]

By mid-1983, McCaffrey and her children were all going full speed ahead. Alec had graduated from the University of Massachusetts *magna cum laude*—with great honors—and was headed for graduate school at the prestigious Massachusetts Institute of Technology in Cambridge. Todd, who had enlisted in the U.S.

Army in 1979, was a sergeant serving in West Germany. Gigi had followed Alec to Boston and was taking classes at the University of Massachusetts. McCaffrey was writing and building up the horse business. In 1984, she expanded and moved Dragonhold Stables to Ballyvolan Farm Upper in Newcastle, County Wicklow.

Leaving the business in the capable hands of its managing director, a woman named Derval Diamond, McCaffrey hit the road again, this time going to Calgary, Canada, to speak at a children's literature conference. She was a little nervous—she did not consider herself a children's writer—but all went well.

Gigi returned to Ireland that year and enrolled in a business college in Dublin. Although she still suffered from the Crohn's disease, she refused to let her illness take control of her life.

The first Pern-based science fiction convention also took place in 1984. IstaCon was held in Atlanta, Georgia, and McCaffrey attended, accompanied by Gigi. There McCaffrey and artist Robin Wood began to plan another joint project, *The People of Pern*, a collection of drawings of Pern's main characters. It would be four years before the book was completed and published. McCaffrey and Wood traded lists of characters to be drawn for quite a while before proceeding to McCaffrey's specific details of what everyone looked like. Sketches went back and forth, McCaffrey wrote and rewrote her thumbnail descriptions of the characters, and the book slowly took shape. McCaffrey was delighted by the final paintings. In her introduction to the finished product, she wrote,

"This woman paints real good. The Dragonlady says so."[5]

By 1985, McCaffrey had built a twelve-stable American-style barn at Dragonhold's new headquarters. People in the area thought her stable was so posh that they nicknamed it the "Horse Hilton." When trainer William Micklem came to work at Dragonhold, he brought the Golden Saddles Young Riders Competition with him. The competition was designed to prove that one could make a living and a good career working with horses. It has been held at the Dragonhold Stables since the mid-1980s, and McCaffrey remains committed to helping young riders. William Micklem's brother John also trains horses.

McCaffrey's commitment to this ideal was not just a matter of lending her stables to the program for a few days. She had found out that one of her young neighbors was on the brink of running away from home. He wanted a career working with horses, and his father did not believe he could make a decent living doing so. McCaffrey hired the boy to work at her stable. He was trained as an assistant instructor for the British Horse Society. After more studies at home and abroad, he wound up with the career he had always wanted.[6]

McCaffrey was always being visited by fans, friends, and family. In 1985, she invited her former sister-in-law, Sara Virginia Brooks, to Ireland. After a second visit, McCaffrey asked her to come live at Dragonhold and manage the house and garden. Brooks accepted, and McCaffrey promptly converted

Horse trainer John Micklem rides Tolemac. This Dragonhold Stables beauty was the first broken-color horse ever to be admitted to the main showing ring of the Royal Dublin Horseshow.

an old stable block into a comfortable apartment for her.[7]

McCaffrey needed someone to hold down the fort at home because she was gone so often. In 1986, she attended five science fiction conventions. By then, she was taking medication for arthritis that would have slowed down a less determined soul.

The year was full, with four books published: *The Year of the Lucy*, *The Girl Who Heard Dragons*, *Habit Is an Old Horse*, and *Nerilka's Story*. *The Year of the Lucy* is one of McCaffrey's romances. *The Girl Who Heard Dragons* is a novella-length tale of Pern. It was later chosen as the title piece in a short-story collection. *Habit Is an Old Horse*, published in 1986, was available only at Norwescon 9, a science fiction convention in Seattle, Washington, where McCaffrey was the guest of honor. *Habit* contained two short stories—the title tale and "Fallen Angel," which was written especially for the convention edition of the book.

McCaffrey completed the manuscript for her novel *The Lady* in November 1986. *The Lady*, a romance set in Ireland in 1970, is packed with all McCaffrey had learned about raising, training, and selling horses there. She also used it to point out that Irish women had almost no rights when it came to domestic abuse. In the years since then, there have been tremendous advances made in women's rights in Ireland, including the election of Mary Robinson as president in 1990.

A trip to the United States in 1987 brought McCaffrey to New Orleans for yet another convention.

She stayed with her friends and sometime consultants, Harry and Marilyn Alm. Although the Alms were aware that she had some psychic abilities, they were not expecting to experience them firsthand.

In preparation for McCaffrey's visit, Marilyn's mother had decided to organize her daughter's somewhat chaotic house. She did a terrific job, and when Anne arrived, the house looked wonderful. The only catch was that Marilyn could not find anything in it. Anne was sitting in the living room one day while Marilyn went on her umpteenth search. McCaffrey watched for a moment and then called out, "Try the desk in the computer room, the back corner." Then she smiled. Marilyn went to look and sure enough, the lost item was found.[8]

McCaffrey also startled her hosts by enchanting their dog. He usually hid beneath their bed when strangers came to call, and he stayed there until they left. Marilyn had warned Anne about this because she did not want any hurt feelings caused by her dog's behavior. Anne merely smiled and said, "We'll see." She then settled herself into a chair in the living room and waited. In a little while, Marilyn left the room to do some chores. To her astonishment, she soon saw the dog standing at the living room door. A short time later, Marilyn returned to the room to find her timid dog happily seated on Anne's lap. It seemed that McCaffrey had a good measure of the special relationship with animals that she often writes into her books.[9]

McCaffrey had not forgotten her plans to write about Pern's origins. In 1987, she turned to her longtime friend Dr. Jack Cohen for technical assistance in writing *Dragonsdawn*. Dr. Cohen is a scientist who has written several books in addition to advising science fiction writers.[10] They met in 1971 and he helped a number of times when McCaffrey wanted to create scientifically based aliens. He took great pleasure in their joint creations, as did McCaffrey.

Even as she addressed Pern's beginnings, McCaffrey was starting another new project at the stable. Dragonhold opened an indoor school, which was much appreciated by riders tired of cold, windy, damp days on horseback. It was an immediate success and is still in use. There were some quirks to be worked out, though. One day, the Irish winds McCaffrey had tried to keep out became strong enough to raise the roof—literally! Her quick-thinking manager, Derval Diamond, attached ropes to the rafters and tied them to a tractor. Every now and then, a stiff wind can still pop all the rivets in the roof. But so far, unlike McCaffrey's dragons, it has yet to take flight.

McCaffrey's generous nature was not confined to helping other horsepeople. In 1988, at the urging of publisher Bill Fawcett, she started writing some books with other writers. McCaffrey worked with younger writers whose work was well liked by critics but who had yet to reach a large enough audience to make a living from their writing. Some people in the industry wondered if she might be taking a risky step—perhaps her readers would buy her partners' books instead of McCaffrey's. She was not concerned about that in the least.

Derval Diamond in action on a horse named China.

She started by writing with Jody Lynn Nye. In 1985 McCaffrey had authorized Nye to write a children's book using her dragons. Titled *Dragonharper*, it is a book in which the reader is given choices to direct the story line.[11] Their first joint effort was *The Death of Sleep*, which was published in 1990. They would go on to write four more books together.

McCaffrey had first met Nye at a science fiction convention, Norwescon, in 1985, although they had corresponded a little before that. Nye had come to the convention with Bill Fawcett to meet McCaffrey and was very nervous. Fawcett went off to look for McCaffrey while Nye checked into the hotel. Nye later recalled:

> *While I waited, I noticed that three people in front of me was a woman about my height wearing a purple pantsuit and a purple slouch hat. When she turned her head, I could see that her straight, shoulder-length white hair was streaked on one side with purple, red and blue. I had no idea who she was, but I was sure she was part of the convention.*
>
> *After a fruitless search, Bill came back alone. He stopped partway into the room, spread out his arms, and cried "Anne!"*
>
> *The woman in purple turned, and in a loud (though melodious) voice, boomed, "Bill!"*
>
> *"Oh, boy," I squeaked into my collar.*[12]

McCaffrey proved to be both "kind and extremely good at helping nervous young writers to regain their voices," Nye said. "I learned a great deal from her on how to refine my craft. She also brought my name and my work to the attention of her vast coterie of fans, who have been just as welcoming as she is. . . . She, and they, gave me a chance. That's the best thing that I could ask for."[13]

In 1987, Anne was attending a convention in New Orleans when she received word that her brother Mac had died.[14] He had been battling lung cancer and had survived one massive heart attack. Mac had worked for the U.S. government for most of his life, and all the flags at government sites in Hawaii, his last home, were lowered to half mast in tribute.[15] In another balancing of death with a new life, McCaffrey's second granddaughter, Amelia Michael Johnson, was born in 1988, to parents Alec and Kate.

McCaffrey next went to work with Elizabeth Moon on a book in the Planet Pirates series, an offshoot of the Dinosaur Planet books. *Sassinak* was published in 1990, and its sequel followed a year later. By the late nineties, Anne would cowrite seventeen books and have the satisfaction of seeing her coauthors go on to great solo successes.

As the 1980s came to a close, McCaffrey came to a decision. Even though the stables at Ballyvolan Farm were only six miles away from her home, they were six miles too many. She hired a local architect and they began to design a house to be built on the farm grounds. The county planners, who had to approve of the plans for any new construction, were amazed by how large a building she had in mind. Irish homes tend to be smaller than American ones. McCaffrey, however, wanted to be able to entertain her usual flood of visitors, and she liked the amount of space she had had in the United States. It was too large a building for the surroundings, declared the county planners. Why not build it into the hillside so that it would not stick out like a sore thumb? they suggested. And that is exactly what she did. Construction began on Dragonhold-Underhill in 1990.

Flying High

McCaffrey began the 1990s in style with the publication of four books—*The Death of Sleep* (cowritten with Jody Lynn Nye), *Pegasus in Flight*, *The Rowan*, and *Sassinak* (with Elizabeth Moon)—along with a handful of short stories and the construction of her new home.

When she was in the United States for the holidays in 1990, McCaffrey visited her son Todd in Los Angeles. While there, she hooked up with writer Elizabeth Ann Scarborough, who was working on a book set in Ireland. McCaffrey invited Scarborough to come to Ireland and stay at Dragonhold.

They had met many years before, when McCaffrey spent a week working with Scarborough on a writers-in-the-school project for the Fairbanks Arts

On book tours, the beloved author signs hundreds of books.

Association in Fairbanks, Alaska. Scarborough was McCaffrey's guide to the area. The creator of flying dragons and exotic skies found herself traveling by dogsled and being woken early to see the unearthly northern lights. McCaffrey even dined on moose spaghetti![1]

In January 1991, Scarborough accompanied McCaffrey to Ireland. On their arrival from the United States, the two writers went directly to McCaffrey's new house, which was almost completed. They both had books in the works and spent their mornings writing. During midday breaks, they began to talk about an idea for a joint venture. Their afternoons were turned over to discussions of this new project, *Powers That Be*, which would be set on an ice world.

The wealth of details on the characteristics of such a climate came directly from Scarborough's Alaskan background and expertise. Both authors took turns writing and polishing, but McCaffrey was the senior writer and gave the final approval. It proved to be a winning combination. Scarborough returned for a few months each of the following two years to write two more books in the series, *Power Lines* and *Power Play*.[2]

In March of 1991, McCaffrey's arthritis finally became a serious problem. It came to a head when she got lost at the Manchester airport, a very large facility. The more she walked, the more painful the arthritis in her knee became, until she finally came to a halt, close to tears.[3] When she made it home, she called for an appointment with an orthopedic surgeon. She had a new knee by May. Ten days after the surgery she was back riding her beloved mare, Pi.[4]

McCaffrey was very pleased with Dragonhold-Underhill, her new home. She sold her house in Kilquade, but she kept the Dragonhold name. (In Ireland, it is not unusual for a house or estate to be given a name, and a home's owners are permitted to transfer the name to another property.)

Gigi had moved back to Ireland for good in November 1990. She found a job, settled in, and began seeing a man named Geoff Kennedy. In August 1992, on Gigi's thirty-second birthday, Kennedy proposed to her. Meanwhile, Todd, too, was busy falling in love. He had accompanied his mother to the 1992

McCaffrey takes her horse Pi (also known as Cherokee Teacher's Pet) out for a ride in 1992.

Magicon, the Hugo Award ceremony, in Orlando, Florida. There he met Jenna Scott, and it was magic indeed. They also decided to marry, setting a wedding date for December 1993.

McCaffrey had her hands full with two sets of wedding preparations and a variety of manuscripts. She was still collaborating with other writers at a brisk clip. Several cowritten books came out in 1993— *Crisis on Doona*, with Jody Lynn Nye; *The Partner Ship*, with Margaret Ball; *The Ship Who Searched*, with Mercedes Lackey; and *The City Who Fought*, with S. M. Stirling. *Crisis* was the sequel to *Decision on*

Doona, picking up the story several years later. The other three books were part of her Brainship series, which began with *The Ship Who Sang*. *The City Who Fought* had a different twist, though: Instead of running a spaceship, the "brain" is in charge of a space station.

All those books, and many others, reveal McCaffrey's knowledge of military tactics and procedures. Her father, the Colonel, had taught her well. She is equally comfortable tucking hair-raising battles and tender love scenes into her books.

Not one to leave the computer idle for long, McCaffrey wrote two more books by herself: *Damia's Children*, part of the series begun with *The Rowan;* and the twelfth book in the Pern series, *The Chronicles of Pern: First Fall*. This is a collection of short stories about Pern's original colonists.

McCaffrey had other irons in the fire as well. She had bought three barns on two and a half acres, complete with millpond, twenty miles from Dragonhold-Underhill. There she and her son-in-law-to-be began setting up the Farriery School. A farrier fits horses with shoes and often makes them as well. Twelve students enrolled the first year. McCaffrey put what she learned of farriery and its history directly to use in "Black Horses for the King," a tale set in England at the time of King Arthur. First published as a short story in an anthology called *Camelot*, it was later released alone as a book.

McCaffrey was happy to set everything else aside for wedding chores, though, and all was ready for Gigi's August 1993 wedding. "I think it was the happiest day of my life," said McCaffrey. "When I turned to see my son Alec leading his radiant sister up the gravel path to the church in Glencullen, I thought my heart would burst out of my chest."[5]

One of the books Anne McCaffrey had in the works then, *The Dolphins of Pern*, was especially close to her heart. She had been to the Dolphin Research Center in Grassy Key, Florida, in 1986 with Gigi and swam with the dolphins there. While dolphins are not telepathic, they do like people and are willing to interact with them. McCaffrey felt strongly that her experiences with them were a confirmation of the dragon/rider relationship she had described in her

McCaffrey loved swimming with Aphrodite at the Dolphin Research Center. She thinks dolphins are the living creatures closest to her dragons of Pern.

Pern books.[6] It was clear to her that she had found the nearest thing on earth to her Pernese dragons.[7]

Todd and Jenna were married in December. Their wedding was smaller than Gigi's had been, but, McCaffrey recalls with pleasure, "just as happy an affair."[8] Their daughter, Ceara Rose, was born in 1994. When *An Exchange of Gifts* was published in 1995, it bore the dedication: "To Ceara Rose McCaffrey—a little tale for a little granddaughter that she may enjoy more when she's a tad older."[9]

McCaffrey still occasionally went to conventions in the mid-1990s, but her right hip was beginning to trouble her. She started to phase out travel. Having attended more than seventy conventions since 1963, she now felt that it was enough.[10] More troubling than the travel restriction, however, was her realization that it was becoming ever harder to go horseback riding. By April 1996, she had to resort to using a wheelchair to get around. Before she could have a hip replacement, the orthopedic surgeon said, she would have to lose some weight. By September she was ready for the surgery.

Six months in a wheelchair had taken a severe toll. When muscles are not in regular use, they become weakened, and McCaffrey's muscle tone after surgery was terrible. Also, her left knee had been troublesome for a while and was not working well at all. Rather than undergo even more surgery, McCaffrey did a lot of physiotherapy and was finally able to walk using only one crutch. Her difficulty in walking was compounded by another problem that had bothered her for years—tinnitus, a ringing in the ears, accompanied by dizziness that affected her sense of balance.

Fortunately, by this time Alec was in residence at Dragonhold-Underhill. He had come for a visit in the summer and realized that all the management skills he had acquired over the years would come in very handy for his overworked mother. He began handling many of her projects and business dealings. Alec's wife and daughters joined him in Ireland in December. Unfortunately, it was the beginning of the end for their marriage. (They filed for divorce in 1998.)

Alec's involvement in his mother's business affairs led to the development of a *Dragonriders of Pern*® television series, and it all started with a kitten: Some friends of Alec's—Eric and Joanna Weymueller—wanted a kitten for their daughter. Alec invited them to pick one out at Dragonhold, where one of the many cats had just had a litter. There they met Anne McCaffrey and chatted about her books. One thing led to another, and by January 1997 they had signed a deal for a television series.

McCaffrey had had many offers to do projects based on her Pern books. Almost every one of her books has been optioned over the years.[11] When something is "optioned," the author is paid a fee by a producer or production company in exchange for the right to develop the story for some form of theatrical production. Just because a piece is optioned, however, does not mean it will ever be produced. Especially in the case of the Pern books, the offers McCaffrey received did not permit her to retain the control she wanted over the content of the script and the look of the dragons. At one point, she turned down an offer of $1 million rather than relinquish control over her creation.[12]

The Weymuellers' company, Zyntopo, needed additional funding to get things started. They chose Grolier Interactive Ltd., in the United Kingdom, as their partner. Grolier had already developed a computer game based on Pern. Still, they needed more money and brought in a third company, Atlantis Films of Toronto, Canada.

In 1997, McCaffrey collaborated with writer Richard Woods and illustrator John Howe on *A Diversity of Dragons*. It became an elegant showcase for all the

McCaffrey helped design her new home, Dragonhold-Underhill.

dragon lore created in the thirty years since she had begun the Pern series. The book also refers readers to the dragons created by other writers, such as Barbara Hamblyn, R. A. McEvoy, Andre Norton, and Patricia McKillip.

Despite her intention not to travel extensively, McCaffrey found herself back in the United States in 1997. It was her fiftieth college reunion, and Radcliffe had asked her to give a speech for her class. She called the invitation "an honor I could not forgo."[13] Alec accompanied her, a role she had come to describe as "mother-minding."[14]

Another honor was in store for her that year. Longtime friend and admirer Harlan Ellison dedicated a special edition of his award-winning story "Repent, Harlequin, Said the Ticktockman" to McCaffrey. Thirty years earlier, when Ellison was editing the groundbreaking science fiction anthology *Dangerous Visions*, he had asked McCaffrey for a story. She sent him "The Bones Do Lie," and it was chosen for the third volume of the anthology. Publication was delayed again and again, but McCaffrey refused to send the story elsewhere, even though she could have used the money. She knew that one of the main features of Ellison's books was that they featured new pieces, not reprints. The third volume has yet to be published, and in 1994 McCaffrey finally used the story, with Ellison's blessings, in her short-story collection *The Girl Who Heard Dragons*.[15]

An additional source of delight was a CD, *The Masterharper of Pern*, recorded by two of her young friends, Tania Opland and Mike Freeman. They worked together, using the song lyrics McCaffrey had scattered through her Pern books and adding new ones. Opland and Freeman wrote and performed the music they and McCaffrey felt would be appropriate to Pern and its harpers.

There was great rejoicing in the McCaffrey household in early 1998 when Geoff and Gigi adopted a baby boy, Owen Thomas Kennedy. He was born February 22, 1998, a day McCaffrey described as the "fifth happiest day of my life."[16] They brought young Owen home on March 17—St. Patrick's Day. McCaffrey promptly knitted a tiny Aran sweater and booties for her newest grandchild.[17]

In July 1998, Anne saw the promotional video for the Pern television series being put together by the Weymuellers in Toronto. There was the title, *The Dragonriders of Pern*, on the classic blackboard slate used when movies are being filmed. "I had a nice little weep of satisfaction because the little handy-dandy scene identifier made me realize this was really truly *all* happening after all."[18] McCaffrey was immensely pleased to be able to get around what she refers to as "Hollyweird."[19] She retained the control she wanted and the satisfaction of knowing that her work would not be twisted to suit someone else's idea of Pern. Her son Alec was delighted to have helped to make his mother's dream a reality.[20]

Work continued in the stables as well as in the house. Although the Farriery School had closed, the blacksmithing part of the operation was going strong under Geoff Kennedy's direction. Horses were being boarded and trained, and shown at local horse shows.

Alec Johnson manages his mother's business dealings with film and television projects and the Internet.

Sadly, in the spring of 1998, McCaffrey's beloved horse Jack had to be euthanized because of illness and old age. A pony named Barney was also put down at the same time for the same reasons. Even though she knew it was an act of kindness for the suffering animals, McCaffrey was miserable. Both horses were buried at Dragonhold-Underhill. Three trees, an oak, a beech, and a cherry, were planted on the grave as a living memorial.[21]

McCaffrey traveled to England that June for a promotional tour, accompanied by a publicist and a chauffeur. Two months later, she returned to England for yet another convention, sharing the spotlight with Harlan Ellison. Four more books had hit the shelves that year: *Freedom's Challenge*, the first of a new series about a group of humans and aliens stranded on a dangerous planet and their struggles to survive; *If Wishes Were Horses*, a short book for young readers, featuring young heroes, horses, and a touch of magic; *The Masterharper of Pern*, the tale of Robinton; and *Acorna's Quest*, the tale of a magical unicorn girl's search for her home world and family. Cowritten with Margaret Ball, *Acorna's Quest* was the sequel to McCaffrey and Ball's hugely successful *Acorna* (1997).

McCaffrey began 1999 with a flourish when the first book of a new series, *Nimisha's Ship*, immediately became a best-seller. Another book in the Rowan series, *The Tower and the Hive*, was published in the spring and began flying out of the bookstores. The third Pegasus book, *Pegasus in Space*, was in the works in 1999 and was released in April 2000.

The topper came when McCaffrey learned on January 30 that she had been awarded the Margaret A. Edwards Lifetime Literary Achievement Award by the American Library Association (ALA). The award is given in recognition of a writer's contribution to literature for young adults. The ALA's International Committee notified McCaffrey that she was to be honored for the Harper Hall Trilogy (*Dragonsong,* *Dragonsinger,* and *Dragondrums*), *The Ship Who Sang,* and the *Dragonriders of Pern* series. The singling out of *The Ship Who Sang,* her personal favorite of her novels, was especially important to McCaffrey, who said it was "the vindication of my choice of 'genre' and the seal of approval that I yearned to obtain from my father."[22]

McCaffrey went to New Orleans in June to accept the Margaret A. Edwards award.[23] At one point, she and another author, a poet named E. Ethelbert Miller, were asked to read from their works. Because McCaffrey hates reading her work aloud, and was familiar with Miller's work, she simply read some of his poems, rather than something of her own. Miller was flabbergasted.[24]

Why is McCaffrey reluctant to read her work aloud? "Possibly because I write for reading, not speaking, the lines—which are sometimes too much to say on one breath. . . . And because I tend to rush a reading, which doesn't improve the text. In some places, early on, there was no special place to read, and you had to contend with people passing by and other distracting noises."[25]

The timing turned out to be especially fortunate

Todd and Gigi congratulate their mother in 1999 after McCaffrey was honored with a lifetime achievement award by the American Library Association.

for the organizers of the 1999 Dragoncon, held in Atlanta, Georgia, on the Fourth of July weekend. McCaffrey went there after picking up her ALA award.[26] She was mobbed by her fans but found that her right hand quickly became too sore to sign all the books that were held out to her. She offered to pose for photos with her fans instead.[27]

McCaffrey was provided with a three-wheeled electric scooter, which served her well because the convention was widely spread out and she was in great demand. She took part in two panels and found herself at yet another award ceremony. To her surprise, she "acquired two more awards—a Dragoncon dragon—I suspect for just being there . . . and the Julie Award (named for Julius Schwartz of DC Comics fame) for a 'lifetime achievement in the field of Fantastic Arts.' . . . So, for a trip that started out to get one award, I came home with three. Not bad."[28]

The next invitation to travel came hot on the heels of the ALA trip and proved equally irresistible. McCaffrey was invited to Florida to attend the launch and landing of the Space Shuttle *Discovery*. One of the astronauts on that mission, Air Force Lieutenant Colonel Pamela A. Melroy, was a fan of McCaffrey's work. She wrote to McCaffrey, "I particularly like your characterization of women. They are not sweet do-gooders or evil temptresses like you see so much in science fiction. They're a lot like me and my friends."[29]

McCaffrey was thrilled and planned to attend the launch, which was scheduled for the fall. At the last minute, however, she became ill and asked her son Todd to go in her place. She stayed home in Ireland and worked on her own launch: another Pern book.

Late in 1999, McCaffrey's son Todd published a book about his mother. *Dragonholder: The Life and Dreams (So Far) of Anne McCaffrey* is a collection of stories about life with Anne, plus an assortment of photographs from the family albums. Anne contributed an introduction and lots of memories.

Decades after selling her first story, the Dragonlady was still flying high.

10

Taking Stock

Since her first story appeared in *Science Fiction Plus* in 1953, Anne Inez McCaffrey has published more than sixty novels and more than fifty short stories. Her Pern series has been translated into twenty-one languages. She has sold well over 18 million books, and at this point her work is almost guaranteed best-seller status as soon as it hits the stores.

Science fiction writing is now dominated by women, a far cry from the early days when McCaffrey was one of only a handful of women writing in the genre. Three fifths of the twenty-five hundred members of the Science Fiction Writers of America are women.[1] The female characters who populate works of science fiction today are worlds away from the helpless female characters of yesteryear, and McCaffrey's work played an important role in that evolution.

Computers far more sophisticated than the ones that played such a large part in early science fiction are now found in living rooms around the world, and people can play computer games that are based on McCaffrey's Pern. More games are in the works, including one that is being scripted by Todd.[2] Anne McCaffrey has said that her son Todd "will be writing Pern stories after I am gone. He is the only one with permission."[3]

In the spring of 2000, McCaffrey was hard at work on her sixteenth Pern book, jokingly titled, she said, "*Pern!* I've run out of other 'dragon' titles—they've been used up."[4] By year's end, the title had become *The Skies of Pern*, scheduled for publication in 2001. Alec looks forward to generating interest in more of his mother's extensive body of work and is building a house of his own near Dragonhold-Underhill. Gigi balances raising her increasingly delightful son with handling her mother's increasingly bulky correspondence, a job that could easily take all day, every day.

Dragonhold Stables is flourishing, with outdoor and indoor arenas and thirty-three fences for the jumping required for cross-country riding. McCaffrey is thinking about adding more horses. She no longer rides, but her love of horses is undiminished.

McCaffrey tells young writers that they have to be readers, too. She advises them to learn grammar and spelling so their stories will be well presented.[5] She believes strongly in everything she writes, in all her

The creator of flying dragons and exotic skies thinks up more stories at home in her office.

characters. "That gives the words more power," she says.[6]

As for ideas for her characters and stories, they are everywhere. "I constantly borrow this grief, that joy, a snatch of history or background; and work out a different story/ending/problem," she says.[7] McCaffrey observes everyone she meets, and she incorporates their eccentricities into her characters. "Those little traits make characters seem real," she explains.[8] Writers can find names, too, all over— McCaffrey finds them, for instance, in television credits, sports pages, maps, the Internet, even typographical errors in the newspaper.

Looking ahead, she says, "My future plans are to continue writing as much and as long as I can . . . watch my grandchildren grow up. Who knows what else will happen? Considering all that has occurred so far, I doubt I'll be bored."[9]

After close to fifty years of writing, McCaffrey could sit back, collect her royalty checks, and admire her array of awards. But that's not her way. She is as strong-willed, resourceful, and outspoken as any of her heroines. The description she wrote of herself many years ago still holds true: "My hair is silver, my eyes are green, and I freckle: the rest is subject to change without notice."[10]

1926—Anne Inez McCaffrey is born April 1 in Cambridge, Massachusetts.

1947—Graduates *cum laude* from Radcliffe College.

1950—Marries H. Wright Johnson.

1952—Son Alexander Anthony Johnson, called Alec, is born.

1953—First published short story.

1954—Father dies.

1956—Son Todd Johnson is born.

1959—Attends first Science Fiction Writers' Conference in Milford, Pennsylvania, and meets her future agent, Virginia Kidd, there.

1959—Daughter, Georgeanne Johnson, called Gigi, is born.

1967—First novel, *Restoree*, is published.

1968—Wins the Hugo Award for Best Novella for Weyr Search; wins the Nebula Award for Best Novella for Dragonrider; first Pern book, *Dragonflight*, is published.

1970—Divorces and moves to Ireland with Todd and Georgeanne.

1974—Mother dies.

1976—Buys her first house in Ireland; names it Dragonhold.

1977—Opens Dragonhold Stables.

1978—Publishes *The White Dragon*, the first science fiction hardcover book to appear on *The New York Times* best-seller list.

1984—Buys a new estate, Ballyvolan Farm Upper; expands Dragonhold Stables; first Pern-based science fiction convention, IstaCon, held in Atlanta, Georgia.

1991—Moves into a home she helped design, Dragonhold-Underhill, on the grounds of Ballyvolan Farm.

1999—Wins the Margaret A. Edwards Lifetime Literary Achievement Award given by the American Library Association.

2000—Television series, *Dragonriders of Pern*®, begins production and is scheduled to debut internationally in late fall, 2001.

Books by Anne McCaffrey

A Selected List

Restoree, 1967, McCaffrey's first published book.

The Brainship series

The Ship Who Sang, 1969
The Ship Who Searched, with Mercedes Lackey, 1992
The Partner Ship, with Margaret Ball, 1992
The City Who Fought, with S. M. Stirling, 1993
The Ship Who Won, with Jody Lynn Nye, 1994

The Crystal Singer series

Crystal Singer, 1982
Killashandra, 1985
Crystal Line, 1992

The Doona series

Decision at Doona, 1969
Crisis on Doona, with Jody Lynn Nye, 1992
Treaty at Doona, with Jody Lynn Nye, 1994

The Dragonriders of Pern series

Dragonflight, 1968
Dragonquest, 1971
The White Dragon, 1978
Moreta: Dragonlady of Pern, 1983
Nerilka's Story, 1986

Dragonsdawn, 1988

The Renegades of Pern, 1989

The Dragonlover's Guide to Pern, with Jody Lynn Nye, 1989

All the Weyrs of Pern, 1991

The Chronicles of Pern: First Fall, 1993

The Dolphins of Pern, 1994

Dragonseye, 1997

The Masterharper of Pern, 1998

The Skies of Pern, 2001

The Freedom series

Freedom's Landing, 1995

Freedom's Choice, 1997

Freedom's Challenge, 1998

The Generation Warriors/Dinosaur Planet series

Dinosaur Planet, 1978

Dinosaur Planet Survivors, 1984

The Death of Sleep, with Jody Lynn Nye, 1990

Sassinak, with Elizabeth Moon, 1990

Generation Warriors, with Elizabeth Moon, 1991

The Harper Hall series

Dragonsong, 1976

Dragonsinger, 1977

Dragondrums, 1979

The Pegasus series

To Ride Pegasus, 1973

Pegasus in Flight, 1990

Pegasus in Space, 2000

The Powers That Be series

Powers That Be, with Elizabeth Ann Scarborough, 1993

Power Lines, with Elizabeth Ann Scarborough, 1994

Power Play, with Elizabeth Ann Scarborough, 1995

The Rowan series

The Rowan, 1990

Damia, 1992

Damia's Children, 1993

Lyon's Pride, 1994

The Tower and the Hive, 1999

Chapter 1. And the Winner Is . . .

1. E-mail to the author from Robert Silverberg, June 5, 1998.

2. E-mail to the author from Anne McCaffrey, April 28, 1998.

3. E-mail to the author from Anne McCaffrey, October 15, 1997.

4. Telephone conversation with Harlan Ellison, July 1998.

5. E-mail to the author from Robert Silverberg, June 5, 1998.

6. E-mail to the author from Anne McCaffrey, October 15, 1997.

7. Ed Naha, "Living with the Dragons: Anne McCaffrey," *Future*, November 1978. Amended by A. McCaffrey. As excerpted in *Authors & Artists for Young Adults (AAYA)*, Agnes Garrett and Helga P. McCue, eds. (Detroit: Gale Research, Inc., 1991), vol. 6, p. 142.

8. Ibid.

9. Anne McCaffrey, "Hitch Your Dragon to a Star: Romance and Glamour in Science Fiction," in *Science Fiction Today and Tomorrow*, Reginald Bretnor, ed. (New York: Harper & Row, 1974), pp. 278–279.

10. Richard Wolinsky and Lawrence Davidson, "Rigel Interviews Anne McCaffrey," *Rigel Science Fiction*, Winter 1982, p. 20.

11. Agnes Garrett and Helga P. McCue, eds., Authors & Artists for Young Adults (AAYA), (Detroit: Gale Research, Inc., 1991), vol. 6, p. 148.

12. Donald R. Gallo, ed., *Speaking for Ourselves: Autobiographical Sketches by Notable Authors of Books for Young Adults* (Urbana, Ill.: National Council of Teachers of English, 1990), p. 129.

13. Reginald Bretnor, ed., *Science Fiction Today and Tomorrow* (New York: Harper & Row, 1974), p. 283.

Chapter 2. In the Beginning

1. Joyce Nakamura, ed., *Something about the Author Autobiography Series (SATA)*, (Detroit: Gale Research, Inc., 1991), vol. 11, p. 242.

2. E-mail to the author from Anne McCaffrey, March 20, 1998.

3. SATA, vol. 11, p. 241.

4. Agnes Garrett and Helga P. McCue, eds., *Authors & Artists for Young Adults (AAYA)*, (Detroit: Gale Research, Inc., 1991), vol. 6, p. 141.

5. Note to the author from Marilyn Alm, October 14, 1999.

6. E-mail to the author from Anne McCaffrey, May 20, 1998.

7. Todd McCaffrey, *Dragonholder: The Life and Dreams (So Far) of Anne McCaffrey* (New York: Ballantine Books, 1999), p. 34.

8. *SATA*, vol. 11, p. 243.

9. E-mail to the author from Anne McCaffrey, May 2, 1998.

10. E-mail to the author from Anne McCaffrey, May 20, 1998.

11. *SATA*, vol. 11, p. 243.

12. E-mail to the author from Anne McCaffrey, May 20, 1998.

13. E-mail to the author from Anne McCaffrey, May 2, 1998.

14. *SATA*, vol. 11, p. 244.

15. E-mail to the author from Anne McCaffrey, May 20, 1998.

16. *SATA*, vol. 8, p. 127.

17. *SATA*, vol. 11, p. 242.

18. E-mail to the author from Anne McCaffrey, May 20, 1998.

Chapter 3. School Days

1. Junior Literary Guild, March 1977, as excerpted in Agnes Garrett and Helga P. McCue, eds., *Authors & Artists for Young Adults (AAYA)*, (Detroit: Gale Research, Inc., 1991), vol. 6, p. 141.

2. Anne McCaffrey, *The White Dragon* (New York: Del Rey, 1978), pp. 65–66.

3. Joyce Nakamura, ed., *Something about the Author Autobiography Series (SATA)*, (Detroit: Gale Research, Inc., 1991), vol. 11, p. 245.

4. *Do You Know the Answers? Public Appearance and Poise at Radcliffe*, pamphlet published by the Student Government Association of Radcliffe College, 1942.

5. E-mail to the author from Anne McCaffrey, August 19, 1998.

6. E-mail to the author from Anne McCaffrey, August 24, 1998.

7. E-mail to the author from Anne McCaffrey, August 13, 1998.

8. Ibid.

9. E-mail to the author from Anne McCaffrey, August 24, 1998.

10. Ibid.

Chapter 4. Off to Work

1. E-mail to the author from Anne McCaffrey, September 15, 1998.

2. Jeff Chapman and John D. Jorgenson, eds., *Contemporary Authors* (Detroit: Gale Research, Inc., 1997), vol. 55, p. 272.

3. E-mail to the author from Anne McCaffrey, September 15, 1998.

4. Joyce Nakamura, ed., *Something about the Author Autobiography Series (SATA)*, (Detroit: Gale Research, Inc., 1991), vol. 11, p. 246.

5. Ibid.

6. *Speaking for Ourselves: Autobiographical Sketches by Notable Authors of Books for Young Adults* (Urbana, Ill.: National Council of Teachers of English, 1990), p. 129.

7. *The Montclair Times*, August 13, 1953, archived at the Montclair Public Library, Montclair, N.J.

8. E-mail to the author from Anne McCaffrey, September 15, 1998.

9. E-mail to the author from Anne McCaffrey, February 5, 2000.

10. Ibid.

Chapter 5. On the Move

1. Joyce Nakamura, ed., *Something about the Author Autobiography Series (SATA)*, (Detroit: Gale Research, Inc., 1991), vol. 11, p. 247.

2. E-mail to the author from Anne McCaffrey, October 28, 1998.

3. Michael Cart, "The Divine Miss M," *School Library Journal*, June 1999, p. 25.

4. *SATA*, vol. 11, p. 248.

5. Chris Morgan, "Interview: Anne McCaffrey," *Science Fiction Review*, Fall 1982, amended by Anne McCaffrey, as excerpted in Agnes Garrett and Helga P. McCue, eds., *Authors & Artists for Young Adults (AAYA)*, (Detroit: Gale Research, Inc., 1991), vol. 6, p. 143.

6. "Anne McCaffrey: Dragonwriter of Pern," *Leading Edge*, Fall 1985, amended by Anne McCaffrey, as excerpted in AAYA, vol. 6, p. 149.

7. David Gerrold, "Anne McCaffrey: A Profile," *Luna Monthly*, November 1970, pp. 7, 11.

Chapter 6. Up in the Air

1. Anne McCaffrey, "Building a World: Notes on the Invention of Pern," from the Random House/Del Rey Pern Web site, <http://www.randomhouse.com/delrey/pern/amcc/article.htm> (March 12, 1999).

2. Michael Cart, "The Divine Miss M," *School Library Journal*, June 1999, pp. 25, 26.

3. E-mail to the author from Anne McCaffrey, February 5, 2000.

4. E-mail to the author from Anne McCaffrey, December 18, 1998.

5. E-mail to the author from Alec Johnson, May 28, 1999.

6. 10. Todd McCaffrey, *Dragonholder: The Life and Dreams (So Far) of Anne McCaffrey* (New York: Ballantine Books, 1999), p. 67.

7. Ibid., p. 67.

8. Ibid., p. 47.

9. E-mail to the author from Todd J. McCaffrey, January 17, 1999.

Chapter 7. Happy Landings

1. E-mail to the author from Anne McCaffrey, January 12, 1999.

2. E-mail to the author from Anne McCaffrey, February 5, 2000.

3. E-mail to the author from Gigi Kennedy, February 10, 1999.

4. E-mail to the author from Anne McCaffrey, February 5, 1999.

5. E-mail to the author from Anne McCaffrey, January 12, 1999.

6. E-mail to the author from Anne McCaffrey, February 5, 2000.

7. Interview in AOL's *The Book Report*, April 6, 1997, <http://www.randomhouse.com/delrey/pern/amcc/TBRtranscript.htm> (March 12, 1999).

8. E-mail to the author from Anne McCaffrey, February 12, 1998.

9. E-mail to the author from Anne McCaffrey, February 5, 1999.

10. Todd McCaffrey, *Dragonholder: The Life and Dreams (So Far) of Anne McCaffrey* (New York: Ballantine Books, 1999), pp. 100–101.

11. Paul Walker, "Anne McCaffrey: An Interview," *Luna Monthly*, November 1974, p. 4.

12. Ibid.

13. Michael Cart, "The Divine Miss M," *School Library Journal*, June 1999, p. 26.

14. Walker, p. 3.

15. Robin Wood and Anne McCaffrey, *The People of Pern* (Norfolk, Va.: Donning Company, 1988), p. 114.

Chapter 8. At Home and on the Road

1. E-mail to the author from Anne McCaffrey, February 17, 1999.

2. E-mail to the author from Anne McCaffrey, February 5, 2000.

3. Robin Wood and Anne McCaffrey, *The People of Pern* (Norfolk, Va.: Donning Company, 1988), p. 8.

4. E-mail to the author from Anne McCaffrey, February 17, 1999.

5. Wood and McCaffrey, p. 8.

6. E-mail to the author from Anne McCaffrey, February 20, 1999

7. Ibid.

8. E-mail to the author from Anne McCaffrey, February 24, 1999.

9. Telephone conversation with Marilyn Alm, May 28, 1999.

10. E-mail to the author from Anne McCaffrey, February 5, 2000.

11. Online conference with Jody Lynn Nye, on CompuServe SFLIT Two Forum, May 3, 1998 and e-mails to the author from Anne McCaffrey, February 24, 1999, and Jody Lynn Nye, March 22, 1999.

12. E-mail to the author from Jody Lynn Nye, March 22, 1999.

13. Ibid.

14. E-mail to the author from Anne McCaffrey, February 5, 2000.

15. E-mail to the author from Anne McCaffrey, February 26, 1999.

Chapter Nine: Flying High

1. Anne McCaffrey, *Powers That Be* (New York: Del Rey, 1993), p. 312.

2. E-mail to the author from Anne McCaffrey, March 9, 1999.

3. E-mail to the author from Anne McCaffrey, March 8, 1999.

4. E-mail to the author from Anne McCaffrey, February 18, 1999.

5. E-mail to the author from Anne McCaffrey, March 8, 1999.

6. E-mail to the author from Anne McCaffrey, April 4, 1999.

7. Robert Neilson, "There Had to Be Dragons in the Title: An Interview with Anne McCaffrey," *Albedo One*, Issue 10, 1996, <http://homepage.tinet.ie/(goudriaan/interview-mccaffrey.htm> (February 23, 1999).

8. E-mail to the author from Anne McCaffrey, December 7, 2000.

9. Anne McCaffrey, *An Exchange of Gifts* (New York: New American Library, 1995).

10. Neilson.

11. Ibid.

12. Ibid.

13. E-mail to the author from Anne McCaffrey, March 8, 1999.

14. Ibid.

15. Phone call with Harlan Ellison, April 30, 1998.

16. E-mail to the author from Anne McCaffrey, March 20, 1998.

17. E-mail to the author from Anne McCaffrey, May 20, 1998.

18. E-mail to the author from Anne McCaffrey, August 13, 1998.

19. Neilson.

20. E-mail to the author from Anne McCaffrey, March 8, 1999.

21. Todd J. McCaffrey, *Dragonholder: The Life and Dreams (So Far) of Anne McCaffrey* (New York: Del Rey, 1999).

22. E-mail to the author from Anne McCaffrey, January 31, 1999.

23. E-mail to the author from Anne McCaffrey, July 8, 1999.

24. Telephone conversation with Shelley Shapiro, McCaffrey's editor at Del Rey/Ballantine, May 27, 1999.

25. E-mail to the author from Anne McCaffrey, December 7, 2000.

26. E-mail to the author from Anne McCaffrey, July 8, 1999.

27. Ibid.

28. E-mail to the author from Anne McCaffrey, July 8, 1999.

29. Letter from Pamela A. Melroy to Anne McCaffrey, reprinted at <www.annemccaffrey.org/BookPages/Pam MelroyLtr.htm> (December 8, 2000).

Chapter 10. Taking Stock

1. *The World of Pern* <http://www.randomhouse.com/delrey/pern/amcc/TBRtranscript.htm> (June 28, 2000).

2. E-mail to the author from Anne McCaffrey, May 28, 1999.

3. *The World of Pern.*

4. E-mail to the author from Anne McCaffrey, February 5, 2000.

5. Joyce Nakamura, ed., *Something about the Author Autobiography Series (SATA),* (Detroit: Gale Research, Inc., 1991), vol. 11, p. 256.

6. Del Rey Internet Newsletter, #72, <http://randomhouse.com/delrey/drindex/72DRINJanuary.html> (March 12, 1999).

7. Paul Walker, "Anne McCaffrey: An Interview," *Luna Monthly*, November 1974, p. 4.

8. Del Ray Internet Newsletter, #72.

9. E-mail to the author from Anne McCaffrey, May 28, 1999.

10. Official Web site of Anne McCaffrey <http://members.aol.com/dragnhld/ANNIE08.htm> (March 12, 1999). [Note: McCaffrey's official Web site is now found at <www.annemccaffrey.org>]

Cart, Michael. "The Divine Miss M." *School Library Journal*, June 1999.

Chapman, Jeff, and John D. Jorgenson, eds. *Contemporary Authors*, vol. 55. Detroit: Gale Research, Inc., 1997.

Dohmen, Teri. "Anne McCaffrey: Year of the Dragons." *Crescent Blues*, vol. 2, issue 1, 1999. <http://www.crescentblues.com/2_1issue/mccaffrey.shtm> (October 31, 2000).

Gallo, Donald R., ed. *Speaking for Ourselves: Autobiographical Sketches by Notable Authors of Books for Young Adults.* Urbana, Ill.: National Council of Teachers of English, 1990.

Garrett, Agnes, and Helga P. McCue, eds. *Authors & Artists for Young Adults (AAYA)*, vol. 6. Detroit: Gale Research, Inc., 1991.

Gerrold, David. "Anne McCaffrey: A Profile." *Luna Monthly*, November 1970.

Hargreaves, Mathew D. *Anne Inez McCaffrey: Forty Years of Publishing, An International Bibliography.* Seattle, Wash.: Mathew D. Hargreaves, 1992.

McCaffrey, Todd. *Dragonholder: The Life and Dreams (So Far) of Anne McCaffrey.* New York: Ballantine Books, 1999.

Nakamura, Joyce, ed. *Something about the Author Autobiography Series (SATA)*, vol. 11. Detroit: Gale Research, Inc., 1994.

Nye, Jody Lynn, and Anne McCaffrey. *The Dragonlover's Guide to Pern*, 2nd ed. New York: Ballantine Books, 1997.

Roberts, Robin. *Anne McCaffrey: A Critical Companion.* Westport, Conn.: Greenwood Publishing, 1996.

Walker, Paul. "Anne McCaffrey: An Interview." *Luna Monthly,* November 1974.

Wolinsky, Richard, and Laurence Davidson. "Rigel Interviews Anne McCaffrey." *Rigel Science Fiction,* winter 1982.

Wood, Robin, and Anne McCaffrey. *The People of Pern.* Norfolk, Va.: Donning Company, 1988.

Internet Addresses

The Worlds of Anne McCaffrey™
The official, most comprehensive Web site
    <http://www.annemccaffrey.org>

The World of Pern
    <http://www.randomhouse.com/delrey/pern/index2.html>

Dragonriders of Pern®
A Fantasy-Fiction Writing Club
    <http://www.geocities.com/Paris/Villa/5116/drmain/index.html>

Sariel's Guide to Pern
    <http://www.srellim.org/pern/>

Index

Page numbers for photographs are in **boldface** type.